SWEET MYSTERY
THE GOD I'VE COME TO KNOW

Sonia M. Carter

Publisher: Luminous Publishing
www.luminouspublishing.com
For bulk orders or other inquiries, email:
info@luminouspublishing.com

TABLE OF CONTENTS

*"Courage comes in many forms,
speaking the truth is just one."*
-Anonymous

PREFACE

"Mom, is God real?" A suspicious child asked.

Mom was on a search of her own, looking for words she deemed right and responsible. With a blindsided and flat expression, she offered, "I can't answer that for you. You'll have to find out on your own."

Disappointed, I returned to the basement, where my search had begun, thinking, *Don't moms know everything?* Apparently, they didn't. I'd been rummaging through remnant boxes of Mom and Moses' yesteryears. There wasn't much left. I looked with admiration at a group of marble paperweights—leftover knickknacks from their previous marriage—then opened a box of books. Moses was a man I had zero memory of, but the box confirmed the stories I'd been told.

Moses

I didn't know my father but that's hardly a headline. The last time I checked, nearly 25% of American youth, all ethnicities included, share this reality. It goes beyond the cliché of a "fatherless home." The experience is one of a blurred identity, a *fatherless life*.

The story, as I was told, was that Moses was an elder in the Jehovah's Witnesses Kingdom Hall. He was loved and adored by most who met him—the ones who didn't know him. Behind his charming public persona, Moses was an abusive and self-preserving monster, ruling with an iron fist, manipulating his way to perceived power. I later learned he lived with PTSD from his military service. Worn out from boxing matches, psychological warfare, suspicions of adultery, and the danger of her children witnessing the mess, mom left the veneer of stability to weather the costly storm of freedom.

My first memory of Moses was shortly after we took the midnight train from a Chicago-adjacent suburb to the St. Louis inner city. Survival will take you to strange places. My mom, along with my two sisters and me, settled into a humble two-bedroom apartment on the unforgiving north side. I was running around playing in a nightgown when he called.

"Hello?" I smiled, excited to hold the beige Trimline phone.

"Hey." His voice sang, mellow and reassuring.

Our conversation was short and shallow. He asked the basics, "How are you?" and "You know I miss you, right?"

At three years old, I was oblivious to our situation. I spun my fingers through the spiral cord and smiled. Moses told me to ask mom for my dress size so he could send a few. I imagined having the lace-frilled collars and puffy sleeves that my baby dolls wore.

"MOM!" I anxiously called out. "Moses said to give him my dress size. He's going to send some dresses!"

"Girl, *please!*" Mom interrupted the fairytale. Moses must've overheard because our call ended shortly after. It would be the last time I spoke with Moses for several years. Life carried on without him.

"I love you," he said.

"I love you, too," unsure that I really did.

"For I know the plans for you, declares the Lord, plans for welfare and not for evil, to give you a hope and a future."
Jeremiah 21:11 ESV

PART I

WIDE IS THE ROAD

Chapter 1 | O Simple One

"If I must boast, I will boast of the things that show my weakness."
2 Corinthians 11:30 ESV

Life was about to sucker punch me, and I had no idea. At eighteen, I was a slightly sheltered and naïve youth full of zeal and imagination. I stood at a crossroads, wondering, "What exactly do I do with this life?" My close friends were off to great colleges. My siblings were into their careers, and there I was, unsure of where I belonged, what I wanted for my life, and feeling lost. My mom shared the opinion of many old-school parents: after high school graduation, you either go to college or work.

Vintage Vinyl was my first real, not so real, job. As the name hints, Vintage Vinyl was a shabby but beloved record store in the heart of University City. Real music aficionados loved Vintage Vinyl for its rare finds, raw culture, live music, and generous promotion of the local talent. Vintage Vinyl, and the Delmar Loop which housed it, taught me just how sheltered I was. I had lived in the community nearly all my life but working in it was something different. I was drawn to the sight of identity expressed authentically, unburdened by the opinions of fearful onlookers.

I'll never forget seeing my first 16" standing rainbow mohawk on a leather-wearing rocker. My mouth dropped, literally. It took Connor, a white bike-riding hipster who wore skinny jeans and black-framed glasses (long before the look was popular) to roll his eyes gently at me to mirror my judgement. In my sheltered world, I was considered an unboxed soul. In this new world, I was the close minded one being critical of others. I was now seeing true diversity, and I loved it. Although I will note, the same environment taught me in its own way, diversity does not necessarily mean unity.

Identity was important to me. Within six months I cut off my permed hair, got mini-twists, and began a hair locking journey. I always wanted natural hair, but in high school, my hair kind of belonged to my mom. Another attribute of some old-school moms. Assumptions and oppressions sometimes come with hair statements. Shorter hair also tends to give a more mature look, and then there's the responsibility of maintenance.

I must also say, there is a common misconception that wearing natural hair means you're culturally conscious or "woke," in a general understanding of "consciousness" or "wokeness." It simply does not. *Looking* a certain way and *being* a certain way are two separate walks. Preferences aren't always intentional statements.

During this time, I took up Muay Thai kickboxing. A local artist introduced me to a title-holding champ who trained and taught self-defense. I loved being in his class and hanging out afterwards. This was a wild bunch, and I was beginning to fit right in. We were from all walks of life: young, old, white-collar, blue-collar, college educated, multi-trade hustlers, dreamers, and of course, a few pretenders. We were a melting pot of folks.

I was still living with my mom, but home was becoming unbearable. Too many individual changes were colliding. Muay Thai served as both my release from the world and my connection to it. Between the record store and kickboxing, I felt alive, or at least sustained. I was morphing into an adult, but while womanhood is assigned to age, maturity comes only by experience.

My first lesson was a man named Duncan. We met briefly at the dojo and later connected at a party. One of our classmates, a photographer, hosted a preview of his collection at a downtown loft space. I was still relatively new to this group, so I stayed near one of the women I had gotten close with. When she went off to enjoy herself, I sat alone and watched an ongoing chess game between Duncan and another guy.

Someone made the rounds with a huge bottle of red wine. I took the large glass of wine, wondering if anyone was going to remember I was eighteen and snatch it out of my hands, but this was the real world, not an after-school special. No one was paying that much attention, nor did they really care. No one was going to force me to do the right thing. I was grown and hanging with good-n-grown folks. As long as I looked legal, I blended.

Up to this point, my idea of a good time had been a bottle of flavored water and a pack of red Twizzlers, but I thought I was ready for more. After half of a glass, I was all giddy and showing my age. I wasn't the kind of young woman preoccupied with appearing older. I was just fine being who I was—an eighteen-year-old figuring it out. Duncan commented with a trace of an island accent.

"You need to slow down; your eyes are starting to droop."

I laughed as only a novice drinker with her first taste of freedom would. Duncan smirked, allowing a gold tooth to emerge. He complimented me on my new short hair, and I noticed his head of locks were balding, our age gap apparent.

Before long, he handed me his phone. "Put your number in here."

I'm not sure if it was the alcohol or a sense of "know-better," but I held his phone for a long while in contemplation. Thinking, "Should I, or shouldn't I? What could it hurt?" I entered my number and grabbed my second glass of wine. Bottoms up.

The next day, tensions were still high at home. There was a standing invitation for me to leave. Although I felt pushed away, I understood my mom was exhausted with single parenthood. She had given a lot, perhaps more than her share, and was ready for freedom. So was I.

Duncan called and offered relief. He was charming and aggressive. Back then, I thought those were great qualities in a man. After small talk, I gave him the spiel that I gave to every other guy. "Do you have a woman? Are you married?" I didn't want to get caught up in unnecessary drama. Based on the night before, I was sure he was single, so I asked out of protocol. His tone surprisingly changed; he was now hesitant and defensive.

"Well, I mean, I'm dealing with my kid's mom."

"WHAT?" I chuckled audibly, "Well, I'm not dealing with you!"

"No! We're not together," he retorted. "We still live together *for the kids*, but it's over. It's been over."

I was sitting in the middle of my messy childhood room folding clothes, trying to make sense of it all, trying to make sense of him.

"Listen to me." He met my silence. "We are not together. Please, just let me take you out for coffee. That's it, that's all I want. Just meet me for coffee. Just one time, that's it."

Ladies! Ladies! Ladies or gents! If this happens to you, RUN. As it's said, there is a difference between *knowing* and *doing*. Logically, I knew better, but I lacked the resolve, foresight, and common sense to support my knowing better. There's no value in unapplied knowledge.

> *How long, O simple ones, will you love being simple?*
> *How long will scoffers delight in their scoffing and*
> *fools hate knowledge?* (Proverbs 1:22 ESV)

"Okay, coffee." I didn't even drink coffee.

My indifference was the catalyst for coming trouble. I supposed his explanation was genuine and I obliged, thinking just one cup would be fine. I had no intentions of commitment.

The next day we met at a coffee shop in the loop. It was an ugly day, cold, wet, and foggy. He bought coffee for himself and offered a cup. I declined. We walked and talked. Casual conversation soon turned into a deeper connection. We related to idealized concepts of spirituality, a mutual rejection of religion, holistic lifestyles, natural hair; the conversation turned to ideas of identity, books, and Muay Thai. He acted impressed by the interests I held for my age. Looking back, I know it was my inexperience that encouraged his pursuit the most.

Based on our previous conversation, I knew he was in his late thirties, but this day he shared that he had two children—a nine-year-old and a six-year-old. The thought of children was daunting for me, I still felt somewhat like a child myself, and these children were approaching adolescence, so we were relatively close in age. Despite the good time we were having, I fully intended to walk away from that day unattached.

Duncan asked to hold my hand. In my heart I felt I shouldn't, but I said yes. After an awkward moment, our fingers interlaced. He appeared bashful and smitten, seemingly having his head in the clouds. At any given moment, he'd look at me and say "Wow," as if he were so enthralled.

This would've been the day to gain understanding. *"So, Duncan—you're living with a woman, the mother of your children, and you two are not together? Explain."* But the whole time I was distracted and indifferent. Prior to our meeting, I convinced myself I didn't care since I didn't plan on sticking around long enough to be affected. A cup of coffee, that's it. But, in actuality, I was quickly getting caught up in something that was indeed materializing.

7

A cup of coffee turned into handholding, then an eventual kiss. What was I thinking? I wasn't thinking—only feeling. Heavy winds blew the entire day to complement the storm I had just found myself in.

> *"So whoever knows the right thing to do and*
> *fails to do it, for him it is sin."*
> James 4:17 ESV

CHAPTER 2 | WANDERING

"Pride goes before destruction,
and a haughty spirit before a fall."
Proverbs 16:18 ESV

We were now something. Duncan called every morning at 5 a.m. before his shift to say, "Hello sleepyhead," again every lunch hour to chat and finally on his way home from the assembly line—faithfully. I wasn't thinking anymore; just feeling. He took ownership of me, and I felt filled by the feeling of being wanted with a firm desire but had no clue I could drown in these waters. As it's said, *feelings have no brains*.

He wasn't like my father, who said he loved me and didn't care to know me. He wasn't like my mom, who I felt saw me as an inconvenience and in the way of her freedom. He wasn't like the boys my age who wanted me only if it were popular or acceptable. I was wanted with a certainty that was validating. I, in return, wanted him more. He was jealous of young men my age who showed interest, so I talked to them less. It was as if he paid the highest price for my affection and won the bid—a short sale of the soul.

9

This, my friends, is what pimps and whores are made of. A predator clever at doing wrong. A lost sheep not knowing the voice of the Shepherd, walking herself to be slaughtered and restlessly calling danger fun. We were feeding each other's voids and insecurities. Mine were more evident; however, he was older and facing his own realities and uncertainties from disappointments and decisions. An eighteen-year-old with little depth perception and life experience would not hold him accountable the way his peers would—thus, I became an escape he used to feed his ego and make himself feel useful again.

One Thursday night after Muay Thai class, I came home exhausted. Mom started yelling about something, fuming through cigarette smoke. I was numb to it all. Every word sort of bounced off of me and fell flat. Not too long into her screaming, she roared those infamous words that I had grown accustomed to, "You can get out!" This time, however, her words awakened me. From numb to determined, *"out"* was my agenda. While she was swept away in her ranting, I started packing. With no idea where I was going, I gathered some clothes, random personals, and a pack of red Twizzlers.

It was ten o'clock at night. I had no car and less than a hundred dollars to my name, but I had to go. I simply couldn't take anymore. I waited until she turned her back, then I went right past her bedroom, through the living room, and out the front door. It had snowed a day prior, not the best conditions for carrying bags on foot, but I didn't care. *Somehow, I'd be okay*—the reckless sentiment of a pseudo-adult without a plan. Mom must've heard the front door close because she was now at the front porch yelling my name. I looked back once; *back there* was enough to validate my pursuit elsewhere, anywhere but there.

When I was more than a few houses away, out of her sight, she called my cell phone. I was convinced that the God I didn't really know was with me. I remember the moon being full and bright, and the light comforted me as I walked the familiar but dark streets. I started writing poetry in my mind to comfort my soul and soothe the frustration.

She called. God called.
I answered the Higher call.

I repeated those words to myself as I slushed through the snow, not knowing what they even meant. I only knew that I needed to go. I thought I was doing something noble for myself, relieving myself from the turmoil. Anywhere else seemed better than the hellish home. But seriously, what was I going to do? In the meantime, I decided to head to the grocery store. On the way, a car slowed down to observe me closer. Another car flashed their headlights and tapped the horn to get my attention. One man actually got out of his car about 50 feet from a park I stood in front of, trying to wave me closer. I was getting freaked out. It was obvious I was in over my head.

I thought of Paul, an older man I'd met in The Loop. He had a heart for the community and told me at least a dozen times that if I ever needed anything, day or night, to call him without hesitation. Although I was convinced that he used his "care for the next generation" as a method to pick up ladies, and he kind of weirded me out, he never tried anything with me so I'd take him up on his offer. I'm sure this wasn't the call he meant.

He worked at the airport, sometimes overnight. When he answered, I apologized immediately and told him I needed to spend a night at his place, no more than two, to figure some things out. This was naively bold of me. Just a typical youth, inconveniencing the world for my troubles, not to mention the sheer danger of it all.

I once watched a testimony of a run-away who was invited to stay with a friend. Her night quickly turned left as she was raped and was just hours away from being sold into human trafficking. With the way I maneuvered, I am blessed to be alive and sharing my story. Paul assured me there was no need for apologies and confirmed he'd pick me up after he got off work at midnight. I told him I'd find somewhere to hang out to bide time and give him the address when he was on his way.

I continued to ignore Mom's calls as I dialed another recent acquaintance. Caesar was an up-and-coming rapper who hung around the record store trying to get a buzz for himself. He'd been trying to take me out for weeks now. I called him and shared a few spotty details. He was at work too, at a downtown Marriott hotel. He said he'd be able to help me out for the few hours I needed. He snuck out of work, drove 20 minutes away, and found me standing in an empty store lot with my overstuffed duffle bags.

As he opened the door to help me squeeze my bags into the back of his '90s muscle car, music blasted my eardrums. He was proudly pumping his own self-proclaimed hits. This was the first time we saw each other outside of my place of work, but I was too tired to entertain any "get to know you" conversations. His energy lifted mine a bit, a welcome distraction, but I was more grateful things were happening perfectly as I planned them.

When we pulled up to the hotel, he had me wait in the car while he checked to see if his manager was away as anticipated. Five minutes later, he returned with keys and a room. He was able to sneak me into a room that wasn't yet booked, but warned that we had to be out by

5 a.m. when management arrived. I was confident we only needed until 1 a.m.

We sat on opposite sides of the bed, both at the head. It was obvious my drama was just that, mine. While I was completely worn out and unsettled, he was high on energy and cracking plenty of jokes. Since he was still on the clock, he left periodically to show his face in the lobby and deliver toiletries as needed. I called Paul to let him know where I was, and he told me he'd call me in an hour when he got off work. For now, I could breathe. At least I had the next 48 hours to figure things out.

Caesar interrupted my thoughts as he reentered the room. I gave a quick update; then we laid back to chill. Well, I laid back, and he leaned in. I wasn't the only one wanting something that night. He wanted to see how far his acts of kindness had gotten him. *Ugh, I just wanted to chill.* Plus, I was sweaty and not in a cute glistening way. I kick-boxed earlier that evening, and without showering had embarked on this impromptu journey.

Through guilt and pride, I decided it was acceptable to barter begrudged kisses for the room stay, so I commenced the transaction. When he started to unclasp my bra, I wasn't with it and pulled away. He seemed only slightly disappointed and appeared almost as mutually disinterested as me. I suppose for him it was worth a shot just to see how far he could go.

14

He clicked on the TV, and things returned to semi-normal. I was too distracted by how my night was unfolding to watch infomercials. Instead, I watched my phone incessantly, begging with my eyes for midnight to come.

The moment midnight struck I called Paul. No answer. "Well, maybe he's wrapping up." Five minutes later, I called again; still no answer. *Maybe, he's leaving the terminal and has bad reception.* I left a brief voice message. Ten minutes later, I'm thinking he's got to be off by now. I called back. No answer. I saw Caesar in the corner of my eye; he was now attentive. I left another voicemail, trying to hide a frantic tremble.

Caesar said, "He's not picking up?" seemingly concerned.

"Not yet, but he will," Me putting faith into a man I barely knew.

By now, Caesar was fighting sleep. A big lump formed in my throat as I realized that my plans were crumbling. *Where is he? Is he avoiding me? Why would he tell me he was coming and then not come? That doesn't make any sense. He's still coming, yeah he's still coming.*

Ten minutes, twenty minutes, thirty minutes later, each time I called back. No answer. After forty-five minutes, I called again; this time, my call went immediately to voicemail. Still, in hopeful denial, I thought, "Either he's ignoring me, or his phone died."

15

Against all I knew, I chose to believe the latter and decided to wait for him to recharge his phone and call back. He wouldn't leave me hanging, would he? My eyes were incredibly heavy from the long day.

I laid down near the head of the bed where Caesar was slumped over, drooling in his uniform. My plans officially failed. Disappointed and out of moves, I allowed myself to doze off. Around 4:00 am I woke up facing the same reality. Holding onto a misappropriated faith, I called Paul back, but this time I just wanted to hear what he would say. The phone rang and rang—he obviously turned it back on—but still no answer.

Caesar woke up from my movement in the bed. "What happened to *your boy*? He never called back?"

All I could do was shrug, "Nope."

"Dang, that's messed up."

I let out a long sigh, feeling stupid. What was I going to do now? I had nothing left to do but call Mom. Mom had a thing about leaving home and returning. She left my grandparents' house at seventeen and always said she left once and never returned. Here I was, out on a limb without a clue. Young and dumb. I couldn't even figure things out for one night. I had no other choice but to swallow my pride.

Mom's voice was low and raspy from sleep. She answered, sounding both concerned and angry. I quickly got to the point, "Mom, I need to come back for a few hours, and then I'll be out by the time you're home from work." Avoiding rejection, I made it apparent I knew I couldn't come back for good. Mom could've picked me apart. Instead, she listened, knowing I needed her. "Fine, Sonia."

Truth be told, if a few hours were all I really needed, why would I even have gone back? A few hours can be toughed out. It was evident I didn't have a clue what to do. I said, "Thank you," and we hung up.

Caesar and I didn't wait until 5 a.m.; we left immediately. Worse than going home and facing mom was facing myself. I felt so small to have left in such an overture only to have come right back. When I returned, after announcing myself, I went straight to my old room and closed the door. I had to make good on my word this time and be sure to be out that evening. We needed space, and although I was ill-prepared to face the world before me, it was time to go.

This time I called my brother, P., who had a wife and two children of his own. I was confident he was asleep, so I left a voicemail asking him to call me back. Calls like this were rare, so I knew he'd call back as soon as he could—a *knowing* based on relationship versus empty hope. At this stage in my life, with a foundation cracked, I was reaching for whatever I could grab, for some semblance of stability.

17

This time I packed more essentials. After a little while, my mom was up and preparing to leave for work. Right as I got into the bed to finally get some real rest, Duncan called with that sweet tone he used every day to say good morning, only today, I couldn't partake. I shared a few details of my night, but to keep it brief, I told him I'd call him when I woke up.

He sounded devastated and asked if I was okay. I took his care with a grain of salt, especially after the night I'd had. At this point, I had no expectations. I was going to figure things out one way or another and wasn't going to ask him for anything. I sensed him wanting to ask why I hadn't called him, but we both knew the answer. After a strange lingering silence, we agreed to talk later so I could sleep.

As Mom was leaving for work, I could sense a mix of emotions, including confusion, surrounding her. She was fed up for a slew of reasons, many having nothing to do with me. No parent is issued a divine moral handbook on raising another human. I knew she was faced with her own conflictions and questions. She loved me, probably felt some guilt, but strongly desired freedom and an empty nest. Lying in bed at my mom's house, I felt the assurance of safety that those previous hours couldn't give me, and I only had a few hours left to enjoy it.

I woke up around noon feeling refreshed for the day ahead. I was grateful Mom was out of the house so I could try to figure things out without her standing over me or me having to whisper. I was back to sorting items that would leave with me versus those that would stay. It was a bittersweet moment, more bitter than sweet.

When P. called back, he held a different view of my situation. He listened as both a parent and a sibling. He knew I shared the fault but also knew that I wasn't a *bad* kid. On the strength of that, he resolved to hear the details later and immediately told me I could stay with him—a tentative situation until things between mom and me got straightened out. Then he lovingly shared choice words with me for not calling him the night before. He would pick me up in a few hours before mom got home from work. His word, I could trust. My brother saved me from some unknown evils lurking in the streets.

I returned Duncan's call and filled him in on the details of my transition. Sounding worried, he asked if I was okay or if I needed anything. I assured him I was fine. He asked if he could drop by later before my brother picked me up, saying he just wanted to see me for a second. Knowing my mom would still be at work, I said sure.

After a few hours, Duncan called for the address. He knew the neighborhood and remembered the street but couldn't pinpoint the house. I told him to wait, so I could run outside and wave him down. To my surprise, his truck was packed to the hood with what looked like all of his belongings. I immediately asked what was going on with him. He told me he had finally moved out and reminded me that he had only stayed there for the children, saying, "I couldn't take being there any longer" and that *it* had long been over.

I felt cornered. We had become *something,* but I had one foot in and one foot out. I was clearly trying to figure out my life. Around this time, Duncan was constantly showing me how serious he wanted to be. I was afraid of that kind of commitment, not to mention being eighteen. He hugged me and asked once more if I needed anything. He said he wished there was something he could do to help, but there was nothing I needed from him.

He reached into a pocket inside of his jacket and pulled out a wad of cash. "Are you sure? You need any money?" I didn't, but even if I did, I knew better than to ask for money from some man. I had only asked for money from a boy once, at a weekend carnival two years prior; it was all in fun to see if he would give it to me. The following Monday at school, one of my best friends told me her mother overheard. I was so embarrassed and could feel the unspoken disappointment. I never did that again.

I told Duncan, "No."

Ignoring me, he began counting money, 'Twenty, forty, sixty, eighty, hundred. Is this enough?"

"Duncan, no. I'm ok." My record store job gave me a sense of security.

"One-twenty, one-forty. Here, please." He held the money out. "Take this, please. I can't do anything else, but I want to make sure you're okay."

Finally, I took the bait. He was showing me a thin veil of security. I was captivated, not by the money alone, but by the whole display of this man hard-pressed to cover me. He pulled $200 from his billfold, giving me 70% and leaving roughly a third for himself. Such a display. He seemed to want good for me. My brother was a generous soul and had looked out for me when it came to money, but from a man interested in me, that seemed like such a huge deal. At eighteen, teenagers didn't have that kind of money just to give away to a crush, nor should if they did. I thought the gesture meant something special. We kissed quickly, and I ran inside smiling.

"Because the daughters of Zion are haughty, walking with heads held high and seductive eyes, prancing along…Instead of perfume, there will be a stench; instead of beauty, branding."
Isaiah 3:16,24 CBS

CHAPTER 3 | MOVING DAY

"Only fools say in their hearts, 'There is no God.'"
Psalm 14:1 ESV

P., is my absent father's son from a previous marriage. Growing up with only sisters, I always wanted a brother and knew there were rumors of one. I met P. when I was thirteen years old in a made-for-TV-movie kind of way. As I remember, his friend lived across the street from us for several years without us knowing. Through word of mouth, he heard that P. might have relatives nearby— our last name was the giveaway. One day, out of the blue, our neighbor asked my mom if she was who she was, and the rest was history.

P. told my fifteen-year-old niece to make room for me. She made me as comfortable as possible, but time would later prove she would struggle between enjoying a new big sister-friend and needing her space to grow. My transition became everyone's transition. A week had come and gone, and my brother's household was barely handling another body in the house.

After a month of living with my brother and his family, I discovered my period was late. Never, in the history of gratitude, was I more thankful than that day to be a virgin. Life was moving faster than I could handle, and the stress was catching up with me physically. When the fun from living with my brother dwindled, I did what I learned to do best and stayed away as much as possible.

Duncan was en route to pick me up. He waited a few doors up from my brother's house to avoid obvious questions. I could feel his excitement as he drove us to his friend's house, where he was now temporarily living. This was the same friend, Shaw, who accompanied Duncan to the loft party. Shaw, a quiet giant, opened the door. I politely took a seat in a sunken fabric chair and noticed how the home lacked any sense of style. It was decorated with dusty bodybuilding trophies, mismatched furniture, and the smell of canine; Shaw owned a Rottweiler which stayed in an oversized cage in the living room. For a short time, the three of us watched television together until Duncan escorted me into his new bedroom.

The room decor matched the living room, underwhelming and depressing. We sat on the floor, as he had no bed, and giggled over nothing. I heard the volume on the TV in the next room dramatically increase; Shaw was giving us privacy. The environment was foretelling and should have spoken volumes. I wasn't listening.

Days later, my kickboxing trainer invited a few of us, including Duncan, to participate in a demonstration. Hosted by a local library, the showcase would promote the training to a small group. These were the days before social media became popular, so marketing to target demographics to expand a brand took a little more creativity—hence the library. The weather was horrible on the day of the demonstration, so we all arrived early to avoid unforeseen delays. With time to spare, a few of us separated to browse book titles.

We were readers, but many of us were arrogant. It was as if we, the few of us considered as so-called *conscious*, knew what others didn't, and—by our estimation—this somehow made us *better*. I've seen this play out in many groups, whether the commonality is academics, status, sports, or religion. I've recognized haughty dispositions based on weak variables like money, titles, reputation, and knowledge.

I'd watch as someone would mention a concept that was supposedly on par with enlightenment. We'd all affirm ourselves, showing in one way or another that we were as informed as the next. A tiring game of, *'Look at me. I, too, am worthy.'* We all are valuable, from the famed to the unknown, but we'll only learn this when we focus less on *who* we are and more on *whose* we are. I hadn't learned that lesson yet.

After the others dispersed, Duncan and I stayed back. His phone was on the table, and I clicked the power button to see how much time was left before the demonstration began. Behind the displayed time was the word, "SET." In the early days of cell phones with pre smartphone technology, one of the few ways to personalize a flip phone was to fill in the preset characters with a customized word. Typically used was a nickname or meaningful phrase like, "Born2Fly," "Hustler01," or "JesusSaves."

But "Set"? Why Set? We thought of ourselves as free thinkers. We boasted about being spiritually attuned and spiritually free. Knowing what we thought we knew, "Set" could only mean one thing with this guy.

"Set?" I said, concerned.

"What you know about Set?" He was now equally impressed and unapologetic.

"That's the devil!" Still waiting for clarity.

"Yeah, I *ain't* scared of the devil. Anywhere the white man wants to keep me from going, I want to be!" He was referencing hell and believed it to be a European construct used for manipulation to keep people in bondage to religion, specifically people of color.

Although it's debatable amongst scholars, from what I knew, the word "Set" related to satan, and Duncan believed it, too. I was no Christian, but I was no satan worshiper either—at least not knowingly. Without understanding any Christian theology, I assumed most Christian believers were lost puppets eating every morsel they were told to enjoy. However, even with my views against Christianity, I didn't understand why Duncan would take ownership of a term he, too, associated with the dark realm.

Despite my lack of religious views and having beliefs borrowed from all over, I had a personal and innate understanding that no matter the label you give a person, place, or thing, it still exists despite the label. Yes, Christians call that place hell, others, the underworld. Some nonbelievers would simply call the workings of a Christian's "devil," "opposition." But label or no label, I didn't want to embrace a place connected with darkness. Duncan, ignorantly and arrogantly, did. I was just as ignorant because I laughed it off with him.

That wasn't the only outlandish thing he ever said. Duncan was bold—so bold that people kind of became desensitized to the mess he'd say. Once, he was telling about how he got into a little bit of trouble when he was in the military. He was accused of raping a girl. I'm not quite sure how the conversation came up, but when it did, he drifted into a rant. He sort of denied it, but I remember not being one hundred percent certain that he didn't do it based on his sketchy retelling of the event.

In hindsight, his recount told me a lot about him. He didn't bother to be more convincing of his innocence.

Two men against one woman—he called her a liar. I didn't probe. I should've read the writing on the wall, but I wasn't reading for comprehension. I was living blindly, avoiding my realities, only existing. I was in a stupor, a functioning stupor. Looking back, that has been the only way I can describe this season of my life.

Chapter 4 | I'll Be Right Back

*"Such stupidity and ignorance! Their eyes are closed, and
they cannot see. Their minds are shut, and they cannot think.
The person who made the idol never stops to reflect, 'Why,
it's just a block of wood!"*
Isaiah 45:18-19 NLT

Intercourse was the furthest thing from my mind. I
use the clinical term because that's what it was to me at
eighteen, *intercourse*. My imagination never surpassed
external touch. I longed for emotional intimacy.

Tired of wasting gas, Duncan looked for somewhere
to park. He pulled into a dark lot with an unlit sign that
read MOTEL. I was a little nervous but understood we
both were tired of hanging out at Shaw's place or in a
cramped car. We scurried through the cold into a stuffy
motel lobby.

The attendant was at the end of the narrow corridor
behind a glass window observing us. Duncan asked how
much a room was, and the attendant said thirty-five
dollars. Duncan maneuvered to pull out his wallet with
his right hand while keeping me tucked under his left
arm. He turned to me, smiling with excitement, then

kissed me on the cheek. The attendant studied us, age difference apparent, and through a blank stare, I sensed his disgust. He may have seen it often. In a few hours we'd be gone, and another young lamb would stroll in with an old wolf.

When we got to the motel room, the concierge's scorn faded into the distance, and warmth hit our faces. Not knowing what to do with myself, I moved slowly and tentatively. Duncan immediately threw his keys on the desk as though we were home. He did a quick once over of the room, then sat on the bed and unlaced his shoes. I took my coat off and fiddled around. He small talked and laughed, easing my spirit while continuing to remove garments. He moved swiftly and with intention. To the bed I went as he motioned me closer.

I could feel both of our hearts racing, but for different reasons. I never imagined what it would be like to lose my virginity, but I was convinced, through tumbling emotions, that this was not how it should happen. He was anxious to conquer. I was curious but more cautious.

I heard a little voice in my head, "Don't, Sonia!" I could feel the continuous thud of his pounding heart. Is this really about to happen? Did I care? We were moving so fast. The voice in my head grew louder and urgent." DON'T. DON'T, SONIA, DON'T." It all felt surreal, but with what felt like seconds to decide, I pushed away. Duncan moved back abruptly as if to show great concern and pretend pressure didn't exist. I felt relieved, like I'd just escaped a bullet by a locked chamber.

Duncan scooped me in his arms and asked if I felt how hard his heart was beating. He said he was so nervous to even think that we were about to *do it.* He resumed a gentler and more genuine demeanor. He held me, smiling like sex didn't matter, and only us being together did. Shortly after, he began getting dressed.

"What do you want to eat?"

"I don't know?" I never knew.

"Chicken?" He said sarcastically, poking fun at our stereotyped culture.

"Yeah, that's fine."

"Okay, I'll grab us a bite. I'm starving." He tossed me the remote then landed a couple of quick kisses, "I'll be right back."

For about 20 minutes, I enjoyed the motel retreat and crisp linens but quickly grew bored. Forty-five minutes came and went. Where did he go? I wanted to be with Duncan, not alone in some motel room. After an hour and a half, I felt agitated, abandoned, and stranded.

Duncan came back almost four hours later with a couple of greasy bags from some chicken joint. He was in high spirits and offered no explanation for the disappearing act. Not even an obvious lie, like "the restaurant ran out of chicken" or having to change a flat tire. Nothing. it wasn't even worth a try. What was I going to do anyway? Storm out? No, we were highways away from my temporary home. Was I going to scream obscenities and say I never wanted to see him again? Maybe, but we both knew better. I took it. I accepted what he gave—some cheap, greasy chicken.

Days after, Duncan would talk about that moment in the motel, "almost *doing it*" he'd phrase it childishly as if it were magical for him. It wasn't exactly magical for me. The escape away from public hangouts was nice, but what was even nicer was the escape from almost losing my virginity. It bothered me how nonchalant I'd become.

We continued connecting over ideologies and not-so-new, new-age thought processes—the power of the mind. Duncan continued to act blown away by my independent thinking, often shaking his head in disbelief at my perceived awareness. While I've always hated mindless trends and traditional molds, much of what he saw was actually me regurgitating another's study. If I had been as aware as he believed, we would never have been.

One night, over an anticipated call, Duncan was telling me about his day. Somewhere in the middle of the conversation, he casually mentioned the mother of his children, then continued on with his story. I was taken aback, although I shouldn't have been.

"Duncan, you said you left."

I didn't scream, but my tone wasn't as warm as it normally was with him. While most people would never have called me passive, with him it was all relative. He was more aggressive and my bark had little bite.

Matching my tenor, he spoke rhetorically and matter-of-factly, "What? What do you want me to say? We have kids together."

I was caught up—a series of one bad decision after the next. Believing poorly pieced together lies; *he's not in a relationship, his living situation was for the children,* and his display of leaving to justify those lies. I should have left at the onset. What did I want him to say?

My only logical course of action was to escort my wayward tail out of the way—which I didn't do. Instead, I only accepted, and at that point he knew I would. He had me. Right-minded and right-spirited, I would have made a prudent, self-serving, and truth-honoring decision. But I wasn't right. My spirit wasn't right. I stayed right where he'd have me. Conversation over. I always ask myself, what was I thinking? But, again, I wasn't.

Now that I was broken down and comfortably situated in a stupor, the stage was set for more. Back at Shaw's, we immediately went to his old bedroom. By this time, Duncan had moved back home "for the sake of the children." Pay attention. People use age old tricks all the time because, within the right incubation—inexperience, insecurity, stupidity, craftiness, isolation, pride, etc.—age-old tricks work. Why reinvent the wheel? The packaging sells itself. From outside of situations, it is easy to see clearly. From within, we're often biased and perceive our situation as distinctly different. But as it's said, there's nothing new under the sun.

We went into that same dark and unfurnished place. Only tonight, I didn't notice the depressing walls or the dust-filled air as before. "Sonia. Sonia, wait." That same small voice as the time before. I didn't want to, but I didn't know how to say no. Somehow, I felt indebted. I didn't want to make him feel misled either—silly me. "Sonia, don't. Don't." My spirit, not exactly yelling but clear and urgent. I didn't want to lose my, but my mind…my mind unclear. "SONIA, STOP." How do I tell him no? He's done so much for me. I felt pressure pushing forward. "Don't, Sonia. DON'T, SONIA. DON'T, DON'T! DON'T." "Don't." With walls collapsed, the voice silenced.

> *Beloved, I urge you as sojourners and exiles to abstain from the passions of the flesh, which wage war against your soul.*
>
> 1 Peter 2:11 KJV

My high subsided, and I was fully aware—on the floor of some dirty room. His eyes, full and victorious. My eyes, low and vacant. He had a light, *my light*. I saw just how much I undervalued it. I didn't truly know its worth until I felt a new absence within and observed a kind of new fullness in him.

What did I do? I was numb. I didn't want to acknowledge my truth. I couldn't handle it, not at the moment. I knew I had given away something I would never get back—and it was deeper than the act. I had squandered and forever lost a pure part of me.

Let no one say when he is tempted, "I am being tempted by God," for God cannot be tempted with evil, and he himself tempts no one. But each person is tempted when he is lured and enticed by his own desire. Then desire when it has conceived gives birth to sin, and sin when it is fully grown brings forth death. (James 1:13-15 ESV).

Duncan wiped the blood from me, and we left. I walked from his truck to my brother's door, and my pelvis throbbed. I was different and paranoid that it would be noticed.

Do not give what is holy to the dogs; nor cast your pearls before swine (Matthew 7:6 NKJV).

A couple of days had passed, and I was back to regular life. In fact, I was seemingly *fine* the next morning. When Duncan and I spoke on our usual appointments, he seemed so full of life, so lifted.

"I love you, Sonia," romantically spoken, slightly convincing.

But what did it mean to be *in love?* Was I in love? Did I love him a little bit? Somewhere inside, I knew I wasn't in love but, as it was becoming a habit, I pushed that subtle voice of truth to the background.

"I love you too." I lied, wanting to believe.

So, there we were, in yet another scattered chapter. Love. It felt good to be loved. I could use some love, but *this* wasn't love.

Shortly after the idea of love was introduced, I had new expectations. I didn't realize I did, but I did. I paid more attention to the things I should have in the beginning. I was unintentionally observing the playact of love from a man whose voice broke a little bit each time he said those words.

After training one night, we were all going out for food and drinks, so we took extra time in the locker rooms to freshen up. By the time our crew reconvened to leave, another fitness group was occupying the room our class had just left. Unlike our typical classes, filled with brute sweat and muscles, this class was bouncy, pink, and cute. I would've imagined the room smelled of floral. Ladies bopped around in pastel-colored elastic, highlighting every curve and crevice.

At the window, front and center, stood Duncan salivating like a thirsty dog in the Mississippi heat. He wasn't shy about his excitement. In fact, when he saw me approaching, he cranked up his performance. Moaning dramatically, grunting and laughing hysterically, as if to tell me, "I'm a free man!" Duncan wasn't free. He was bound by lust and pride.

Interestingly, the other men in our group noticed the ladies and smiled but also appeared slightly put off by Duncan's overtures. Some will say, "*Girl*, that was just a man being a man," but I'd seen men look at beauty with respect. Not just a one-off, several men—they exist. There exist men who avert their gaze so as not to give the wrong impression or solicit an invitation, to avoid confusion of intention, or to honor personal convictions. In a world of objectification, these men deserve acknowledgment.

I was disgusted, and honestly, a bit hurt. "Is this what love looks like?" The obvious answer is no. We were not in love. I'd gotten myself in a mess and was lacking deep clarity. I felt disrespected—but did I have a right to? He pursued me. But did that even matter? He was the one saying he'd fallen deeply in love. But so what? Here's the hard truth I learned the hard way. Many people, places, and things that aren't good for us will pursue us. It is up to us to navigate and participate in our own lives so as not to become our own casualties. I didn't get that then.

Duncan and I, no matter the mess of the gray area, were not committed. I'd allowed myself to become a toy. What else do you do with toys besides play? There is no such thing as developing a fruitful relationship structured on lies, lust, fornication, and the like, so how can one then expect a respectful or respectable experience? There is no such thing. You can't plant poison and expect to yield fruit.

But that night, all I knew was that he said he loved me. Beyond Duncan, when it came to *love,* I didn't ask for what I needed, nor did I even know what I needed. I was entirely too nonchalant with life and generally went with the flow, gave what I chose, and accepted what I was given. I did not use my voice enough. Even babies communicate when they're in need. I disregarded the value of my voice.

Among our group was a woman who came around from time to time for events. I didn't know her well, but she was nice enough. We spoke once, maybe twice. In our brief encounter, I couldn't help but notice her beauty. She was what society considers a natural beauty with classical features and storybook hair. Quickly I learned more from her suitors. A few men in class discreetly obsessed over her. Through secondhand whispers, I learned she was in her mid-thirties, had a young son, and would train more if she didn't work so much.

It was at another training demonstration when I noticed Duncan talking with the beauty for a while, and he kept looking my way. He was the friendly type, and for all I knew they had been friends long before I came around. Despite their obvious enjoyment, I didn't think much of their conversation. Not until a few days later.

During our usual pillow talk, Duncan was recapping the night of the recent demonstration. We chuckled over randomness, and then, somehow segueing, he mentioned Beauty.

"...she's just like one of the guys."

"Oh yeah," I conversationally agreed.

"Yeah, I like that. She's down to earth. The other night, I was trying to use you to get off, but you're just so young that I couldn't, so I used her."

Seriously Duncan? I couldn't believe what he was saying. He was now just twisting me in any and every way to see how much I would take. The same man who was jealous of me hanging out with guys my own age told me he used another woman for fantasy because *I wasn't woman enough*. Truthfully, until meeting him, I never desired to be *woman* enough for anyone. I was okay being a typical teenager, not preoccupied with being some man's fetish. I was in over my head.

By now, you're probably not surprised that I didn't choose choice words or *finally* end this toxic situation. The stupor was strong. Half dumbfounded and half careless. I sat silent. Before and after Duncan, I've had a mouth that I haven't always been proud of. But with Duncan, it was as if I was spellbound. It was spiritual, having nothing to do with looks or things. I was in a soul tie. I was lost in what we were when, in reality, we were nothing. Nothing more than an illicit connection based on perverse attraction and secrecy, the breeding ground for spiritual attacks, decay, blindness, and bondage.

I truly lost my way with Duncan. I was quickly slipping without ever pumping the brakes. I willingly sat in the passenger's seat of my own life. Now, we were supposedly *in love* but somehow conversing about a woman who aroused him in ways I couldn't because of my age. *What a pervert,* I thought. Perversion, by one definition, is "any of various means of obtaining sexual gratification that is generally regarded as being abnormal," i.e., a man taking the virginity of a young woman he basically sees as a child.

Chapter 5 | I Just Want to Go Home

"Can a man carry fire next to his chest
and his clothes not be burned?
Proverbs 6:27 CSB

It was a Monday night. I remember because the record store stayed open until 1:00 a.m. every first Monday for new releases. Although I wasn't normally assigned this schedule, it was only fair that from time to time I share the late-night responsibilities. Around 11:00 p.m., I was planning how I would get to North County from U. City since the last bus had already stopped running.

After a somewhat quiet mood, a rush of customers came in. I could tell by the liquor-laced chatter shuffling in and out that the local bistros were closing. I checked the clock; it was after 11:30. I exhaled exhaustion and inhaled a bit of strength to get through the end of my shift. Apart from being tired, I didn't look my best either. It was one of those "throw-anything-on-and-rush-to-work" kind of days. I wore an ankle-length fleece skirt, a random buy that normally complimented my unusual style, but tonight it only dated it. I also wore Oxford-like bowling-style shoes that, when styled right, would say "fearless fashionista," but tonight it screamed "fashion faux pas."

I was gathering CD sleeves between pointing customers in the right direction when in came Duncan and Shaw. Usually I'd be excited to see him, but I was worn down, and even worse, my appearance echoed the feeling. Having him see me like this, I cringed for a moment, but when Duncan saw me, out came that gold tooth, waving hello.

"What's up, beautiful?" With a wide smile, he greeted me the same way he always did.

"Hey, what's up?" Respecting my job, I reciprocated a quick hug and waved hello at Shaw.

"You look good!" Duncan whispered in my ear with salivating noises.

It was obvious he'd been drinking. I looked horrible, plus his eyes were bloodshot red, and low. His flattery didn't work. Shaw separated himself, as he always did, giving Duncan space and showing respect.

"What time you off?" Duncan inquired.

"One."

"You gotta ride home?"

"Nah, but I'm gonna ask a friend." Not wanting to share that I would probably catch a cab.

"No. I'm going to take you home. I'll be back when you get off." I thought I liked aggressiveness.

I was so grateful I didn't have to figure it out that night: no cab, no wasted money, no wait. I was a bit of a night owl, but this particular night all I wanted to do was go to my brother's house, curl into a ball and rest. I was past exhausted.

After the last light was turned off it was 1:00 a.m., I ran outside to a pair of taillights that I knew belonged to Duncan. I opened the door and crawled in headfirst to give an endearing kiss, then plopped down and buckled myself in. Duncan was smiling, telling me how happy he was to see me. I was happy, too, but too tired for much interaction. Duncan knew the route to my brother's house, so I laid back and relaxed while he drove. I was so grateful I didn't have to worry about finding my way home.

After a while, I noticed we were detouring. I sat quietly in the passenger's seat, wondering where we were going. I trusted he'd take me home as he had before. We rolled into a dark parking lot. Once the car eased onto the blacktop, I saw the dimly lit, shabby sign: MOTEL.

My heart dropped. Never mind the fact that he told me he was taking me home, that he knew my expectations this night, or that he didn't bother to ask me. Never mind that I was so tired, I just wanted to go home. I was agitated, but there I was, silent. I didn't want to say anything. After all, he did offer to take me home. Logically, I knew the ride home shouldn't have mattered, but I felt guilty. Guilty and indebted that I wasn't stranded at work. But now, I was stranded at this motel.

Duncan didn't introduce any details. When he turned off the ignition, we both got out of the truck, on cue. I was turned off by his inconsiderate behavior and grew more and more irritated with each yawn. But still, I said nothing. What happened to the spitfire others knew me to be? I was in a stupor that I couldn't shake, a dangerous stupor. I use that phrase a lot. It's the only way to describe those days.

Duncan bought a room and was handed the key. I don't remember any conversation. It was late, and I drifted in and out of conflicting thoughts of anger and my complicit nature. The door to the motel was tagged with graffiti from the street side. I suppose it set the mood for what was to come. Once inside, Duncan threw his coat on one of the twin beds and used the seedy bathroom ahead of it. I sat on the opposite bed, slumped with my head into my palms. I was so tired.

When Duncan came out, his pants were off. It was obvious what he wanted, but tonight I didn't want to. By now, we'd had sex twice before. The first night on the dirty carpet and another forgettable time. I wasn't sure if I liked sex enough to make it a recurring pastime. Not like this. Duncan was now in front of me and a bit different from the Duncan I thought I knew. He still smirked and giggled but was more abrasive, more mechanical than before. Instead of serenading me, he moved like he had a job to do, and I was on the clock.

I don't want this anymore, I thought, but I couldn't muster the willpower to say it. To say ANYTHING. *Speak, Sonia, speak!* Three thoughts rotated in my mind: *I'm so tired, he said he was taking me home, and why would he bring me here?* A rhetorical question, of course.

In and out of thoughts, I watched my skirt was being pulled off. Duncan stood over me while I sat on the edge of the bed. His stare was chillingly cold. This wasn't like "us"—there was no connection. He was focused solely on one thing, and I wasn't cooperating. I was fussy and whiny. Like a child, I needed a nap. But I was grown and complicit. I could see Duncan growing impatient. I was disappointed in him and how selfish he was. I didn't want to give of my body, and still, somewhere in me, I didn't want to disappoint him.

He pushed me back and proceeded to push through. Even the night I gave away my virginity was easier than this night. The more he pushed, the more I pulled. Physically, I couldn't take the pain.

After growing tired of toying with me, he said in a low tone, "Open your legs,"—continuing to push. All I did was recoil in painful moans and ouch-like sounds, unable to say no. *Speak Sonia, speak.* To this day, I have no idea why I didn't just scream, "Stop!" It was as if I couldn't. I scrambled to get away, but he held my legs to keep me from inching back. We all know the rule: you have to say, "No."

Did he think I was enjoying myself? I remember expecting him to just stop after seeing my discomfort. When he saw me turn from pain, surely he'd be turned off. After all, he said he loved me, and at the very least we were friends, right? Who wants to bruise their friend sexually? Who wants to have sex with someone who seems uninterested, or worse, disgusted? How was he still in the mood?

He didn't care, and I learned very quickly how little I knew about him, sex, love, and my limitations. If someone had told me six months prior that this night would be my reality, I would have been in complete disbelief. I thought I was entirely too strong, too good, too bright, for this to happen to me. If someone would've shared this experience as a secondhand story with me, I would've offered all kinds of simple solutions and exit routes. But there I was, entangled in a net, without a clue.

After another painful attempt, I screamed *out,* "AHHH!!!" I was over this. He was, too. My lack of participation was interrupting his impromptu release and prolonging his scheduled quickie. What seemed like forever to me had only been minutes.

Speak, Sonia, speak! My only response, moans of pain as he pushed. Surely, he could see my pain.

"OPEN YOUR LEGGGGSSSSSS!!!!!!!", he roared. It froze my body and frightened me into reality. Just like a movie scene, the sound ceased. Literally. Time slowed long enough for us to catch eyes. Not iris to iris, but this time spirit to spirit. Enemy to betrayed. Everything changed.

This night, I met Duncan for the first time, and he knew it and didn't care. His glance was unapologetic and evil, as if to say, "Yeah, you see me, so what?" That moment messed with my head. I was officially tired of the tussle and gave in for the taking. He succeeded.

In my mind, I yelled and cursed to no end. I wanted to fight, scream, and cry, but all of these were active responses. I laid complicit and dormant. My voice had long been silenced. It was still there, but unused. I had given away my power and chosen victimhood. Inside I was angry with him but didn't permit myself to display it. I was even more upset with myself.

My heart was shocked and scared of what I was witnessing. I had never seen this Duncan. I felt violated, with my own help, of course. I helped him bait me. With the exception of a rhythmically throbbing pelvis, I laid defunct. Duncan was completely okay with going to town on a lifeless body.

Just then, the strangest thing happened, the most bizarre, out-of body experience. I was looking down at myself from the ceiling in the corner of the room. I saw myself checked out. He was plugged in, ramming a rag doll, serving solely himself. I felt sorrow for her, lying there stuck in her own space and time while life was happening to her. How was I watching her, me, from above in the corner of the room? How was I seeing my own face?

I later learned the experience is called "dissociation," which can be loosely defined as a disconnection caused by stress, illness, or trauma. I'd never experienced it before or after. I don't remember anything that night following that moment. How we interacted, if we interacted. Did he open my car door like before? Did he hold my hand on the drive? Did we kiss goodnight at my departure? Did I speak to anyone once I got to my brother's house? What time did I get in? I don't know. I don't know.

I do know I pulled myself together as the days came and went. I was always considered strong amongst my peers and that's what strong people do, pull themselves together. If onlookers could've been a fly on the wall, they'd have seen just how weak I was—walking blind, overstepping purpose, true identity, and to my surprise, lacking self-worth. Why was I so lost? Being so weak? So polite? So frustrated? So unable to get it together?

After about a week of going through the motions, while at work, it happened. Out of nowhere, I broke. Alone in an employee-only area, I erupted—thunderous bursts of tears, without warning. I couldn't contain myself or think clearly enough to run to privacy. My wounds were exposed. I was gasping for air through snot and squeals.

Kat, an older coworker, happened to be passing by and yelled, "Are you okay?"

Through bloodshot eyes, I looked up and lied, "Yeah." I ran outside, tears falling uncontrollably.

Across the street from Vintage Vinyl, in front of an old apartment building, there was a small grassy area with a couple of park benches. I sat alone, needing to finish the release. I mourned for my ugliness. I mourned for my participation. I mourned for my complicities, for my confusion. I mourned for my waywardness, my state of apathy, my hopelessness. I mourned the constant feelings of rejection and my not-good enough-ness. For not having it all together. For seeming so lost in life and feeling like a failure. *I mourned because a part of me was gone forever.*

Midway through my sobs, I saw a disheveled old man slowly walking by, pushing a cart. He looked dreadfully concerned. I rolled my eyes as if to warn, "Leave me alone." But I couldn't stop crying long enough to portray a real threat.

The old man's face looked as though his heart was breaking. He cautiously walked towards me. Still sobbing, I grew equally agitated and curious. What was he doing? I was obviously having a moment here. He stopped a few feet away and spoke. His words were stressed, definitive and consistent, but foreign—perhaps a European accent? I wasn't sure.

He continued to speak indistinctly as he sat on the opposite end of the park bench. My annoyance turned into amazement when he reached his arm out in my direction and continued speaking in his foreign language. His face was distressed, but his presence was now completely comforting. I continued lamenting with even fuller wails. I needed it out of me. It was one step towards healing.

How could I have been so stupid? Just a few years earlier, I remembered that I vowed amongst friends not to have sex before marriage. *I truly believed I would wait, and I held the belief without having any religious conviction.* It just made sense to me. But there I was, looking at myself and hating what I felt I'd become: a leftover, maimed piece of meat.

That day, I yelled into the atmosphere, *"I will never forgive myself."* I spoke this, cowardly, half talking to a God I barely knew. I didn't have to worry about whether or not God would forgive me. I didn't forgive myself, and I was doing us both a favor. Without formal religion, I'd always completely believed a God existed. An innate knowing. As thoughts of God and His presence surfaced, I quickly interrupted saying, *"I don't care if You forgive me;*

I will NEVER forgive myself!!!" My words released a curse against myself that would confront me later.

After I was all cried out, I turned to the kind stranger who was patiently looking on. Through a cracked voice, I thanked him and walked away.

"For the one who sows to his own flesh will from the flesh reap corruption, but the one who sows to the Spirit will from the Spirit reap eternal life."
Galatians 5:19-21 ESV

CHAPTER 6 | MAKING A DECISION

"I was ashamed and humiliated
because I bore the disgrace of my youth."
Jeremiah 31:9 HCSB

Spring had come. It was March, just months from my nineteenth birthday. After my needed breakdown and a couple of days processing thoughts, I *finally* made a decision, one that took no internal convincing, no pleading, no bribing. The decision felt made before I acknowledged it. We were done.

That evening at work was a quiet one. The store was perfectly staffed for the few customers that browsed the shelves. I examined my decision all day and decided that I'd make the call to dissolve our messy situation-ship as soon as I took my break. When lunchtime came, I honored my decision and ran to the attic of the store, which doubled as our break room. Although ready, I was unsure of what to say.

Duncan was waiting for my call, and lunch was only 30 minutes, so I decided to just wing it. The phone rang twice before he answered. He could sense something was off. What's crazy is that we were in such an inappropriate and dysfunctional situation-ship, but he only understood there was an issue because I had been uncharacteristically avoiding his calls.

"Duncan, I can't do this anymore."

This was a loaded phrase but included being a dummy, a lost sheep, a toy, a side chick, and a fool.

He saw it coming. I interrupted his silence with a small explanation to reaffirm my decision when he began to sniffle. Is this man crying? He cried uncontrollably, spouting out broken phrases. I was completely confused by his reaction. His tears were telling.

Duncan was dealing with his own issues of rejection. He didn't really love me, of course; he was using me to cover the void of not being good enough, man enough, cool enough, or whatever enough in his own world. I can't speak for him to truly know, but those tears may have been simply because something was snatched from him, presenting the feeling of loss of power. In awe at the turn of events, I held the phone. I felt like someone had cleaned the looking glass. The spell, broken. The stupor, released.

His issues hadn't become apparent because of the vulnerable, or calculated, tears. I believe he was, on some level, emotionally attached; we were in a soul-tie. His issues were revealed by his oblivion, greed, selfishness, lack of control, lust, and questionable sexual behavior.

There was a lost part of him that considered me a friend and an outlet. Now it was gone. I couldn't stomach the call any longer.

"Okay. I'm going to go now." Click.

After a reckless three months, I walked in new clarity. Whatever blockage I'd been experiencing that prevented me from speaking up seemed completely broken off. I had allowed so much of me to be perverted and decayed by the rotten union with Duncan. Suddenly, I saw and spoke clearly, without excuse, apology, or emotion. Suddenly, I did what I knew was the right thing to do. I can't help but think about that little old European man who comforted me in the park. I believe he prayed for me.

A few years later, a woman with proven prophetic insight kept alluding to, then later asking, if I had been raped. I had not. Not in the legally admissible way. I had indeed been preyed on, misused, and vandalized. I, however, aided in my own assault. Words are powerful and, for some reason, I never said *no* to Duncan. I just couldn't get it out—two tiny letters, one life-changing word. To process my thoughts, I wrote.

Sonia M. Carter

I'd Never Call It Rape

No, I'd never call it rape; It was more like

Not enough give and too much take

And although I said it was okay, he was twice my age.

He should've known that shoulder shrugs

Weren't enough to be considered consent.

He should've seen that my hips were only a

Quarter percent of complete development.

He should've stopped when I screamed—

Instead of hushing me, before rushing me.

But ultimately, he was a complete gentleman.

He took a towel and blotted the blood from me.

And I—

I should've left when he left me stranded.

Alone in some motel for four full hours without a phone call...

He said he'd be right back.

And, having common intellect, I should've made the connection.

When he said I was too young to be used for fantasy

to bring him past erection to ejaculation.

He shared how he settled on thoughts of a local model,

One I knew...

And, No

I wasn't trying to wreck a happy home.

When we met, he said it was over

He said he left

And wasn't living there anymore

And No

I wasn't trying to be grown

Eighteen and still a virgin

I was just looking for love

Instead, I found a trap, a lie

The perverted version of…

He was everything I abhorred

Nothing to be desired.

"you are so special."

"you understand me."

"you make me happy."

That's what he told me before he said he loved me

And the way he said it, I felt it.

I mean, I truly believed.

And, I know!

How dumb could I be?

He, sixteen years my senior

Me, only nine over his oldest

He wasn't looking for a wife

But then again, who was talking marriage?

We weren't that concrete.

He kept my mind entangled in

Over-intellectualized accumulations

Eye gazes to chart constellations—

He was so deep

He spoke of the alignment of us, the orbits of love—

He was just so deep

So deep, but never concrete

After he hustled my rubies

My diamond inlaid, my encrusted sacred

I just lay. Naked.

I mean for months thereafter, naked

Fully clothed, but naked.

Bathing this unfamiliar naked.

A distasteful, nothing graceful about it

Naked.

Nothing appealing. This embarrassing,

Self-shaming, naked.

But he told me he loved me

He said it. Come on?

With his sly wicked smile and hand-me-down charm.

Afterward,

I could still feel the energy of a forced phallus

I walked & I remembered

I walked & it lingered

My virginity, I mourned her.

So,

While he preyed on a young-green-grown, pseudo-adult

While he carefully calculated bubblegum smiles

With wit sharp, carved graffiti through kiss

While he performed vignettes of tears, stealing shows

While he screamed, "Open your legs!!!!!!!!!"

As reflex would have them close.

No,

I would never call it rape.

For it was my partake, my subtle curiosities

My willingness to be an accomplice.

And, while I bore the pains alone

Like birthing a stillborn in an alley

I'd never call it rape.

While I arrested myself and tried myself

For what I allowed, I hated myself

I would never call it rape.

PART II

REDEEMED

CHAPTER 7 | A PLANTED SEED

"…so shall my word be that goes out from my mouth;
it shall not return to me empty,
but it shall accomplish that which I purpose,
and shall succeed in the thing for which I sent it."
Isaiah 55:11 ESV

I was at the record store restocking shelves when my back pocket vibrated. I pulled out my cell phone to see a missed call. To my surprise it was Quint. I met Quint shortly before meeting Duncan, but we didn't stay in touch and later reconnected after the entire *Duncan fiasco*.

So, let's go back. My first encounter with Quint, an artist who went by the name God One, was on track seven of an early album. A hip-hop-loving friend had introduced me to a 1990s group called *Chozen Prophetz*. Although I worked at Vintage Vinyl, I'd never heard of these hip-hop pioneers, so I studied with a listening ear. *Chozen Prophetz* talked street life, politics, the role of the man, the need for family, and spirituality over those simple cadences that were so revered in the early '90s.

A track called *'Earths'* was the soundtrack for the moment. Flutes preluded a rhythmic sermon. The group's frontman was a wordsmith who wove philosophy with melody. I studied the lyrics and intonation, wanting to understand the mind of a man who seemed so remarkable and rare. In the three-minute recording, he seemed to get *it,* what others didn't. To have already learned what I desired to know—*Oh my soul, if I only knew then what I know now.*

Days after hearing the track, I asked a coworker, KJ, if he was familiar with it. Every genre in the store had a go-to person, from Jazz to Electronica, Ska to Rock-n-Roll; there was someone for each one, and KJ was our resident hip-hop head. He furrowed his brow and asked me to perform a rendition. I pieced together what I could remember.

KJ browsed the store's catalog system but came up short. "Nah, can't say that I do." I continued gushing over how much I loved the wordplay, the artistry, the hook. I couldn't get the track out of my head.

Two weeks later I was standing at the front registers with KJ who was cracking jokes while we waited for customers to approach the check-out. A couple of guys walked in; I gave a generic greeting but paid them no mind. KJ, who was leaning against a wall with one leg propped behind him, tilted his head and squinted long and hard.

"Sonia, that's God One. That's who you've been talking about—the *Earths* rapper."

I hadn't seen God One outside of a grainy photo on a worn CD insert. I thought it was the biggest coincidence. What were the odds that I'd randomly hear a decade-old album for the first time, talk about it incessantly, and then the lead artist—from another side of the country— walks into my work, all within two weeks?

"Yup, that's him…," KJ verified, "…let me introduce you."

KJ approached God One while I paced the small space, thinking about what I would say. The two had a quick chat, then headed in my direction.

"Hey, One," KJ said, imposing a nickname on him, "This is Sonia. Sonia, this is One." Then he ran off to take care of a customer.

"Hi," I spoke, slightly nervous.

"Nice to meet you." One spoke low, leaning over the counter.

All I could think was that I didn't need this man getting the wrong idea about whatever KJ may have inadvertently insinuated, so I blurted out, "Look, I'm no groupie!" Then a little softer, "But I love your song, *Earths*."

"Thanks, I appreciate that," he smiled, fumbling over a stack of flyers.

Having previously interned at a small marketing and promotions company, I'd been around a few celebrities, wanna-be celebrities, and the culture their status created.

I wasn't about the groveling that's so commonplace. At this point I hadn't met Duncan yet and he'd be the closest I'd ever come to being a groupie.

Vintage Vinyl, being a musician's gem, had a reputation that preceded itself. One shared that he was in St. Louis on business but had stopped by to check out the store before his flight out. The man who walked in with him constantly gave him the side-eye, seemingly frustrated and ready to go. One motioned for another minute. The guy cut his eyes as if to say, "Make it quick."

"Look, I gotta run, but can we exchange math and keep in touch? I'll be back in a few months—maybe we can catch up then."

He was asking for my number. *Math* is a colloquialism commonly used by many in the old school conscious (or enlightened) community. As I understood, it originated with a group called the Five Percenters—an offshoot religion from the Nation of Islam. *Math* referenced the universal laws and principles that governed life, also known as supreme mathematics. One was a Five Percenter.

"Yeah, okay," I acted cool but was freaking out. Is this really happening? I had been learning about metaphysics, the power of the mind, and the ability to forge our own paths with sheer meditative energy and self-will. Meeting One seemed to be a complete manifestation of what I was learning. Was it happenstance? The sum of meditation? Or fate? I had no idea but saw it as more than a coincidence. I was ready to embark on the journey to wherever it would lead. With numbers exchanged, he departed.

So, there I was, looking at my phone, surprised to see his name on the screen. For several months after our initial meeting, I never heard from One. I found it strange but no stranger than in the manner we met, so I didn't pay it much mind. Now he had left a voicemail inviting me to sit with him at an upcoming charity basketball game in my city. Of course, I'd attend.

On the day we met, I wore a boho baby doll shirt that covered my belly and low-waisted jeans frayed at the hips, a nod to the early 2000s. I took the MetroLink transit from U. City to downtown, picked up my ticket from will call, and walked into the stadium, inviting the unexpected. When I found my seat, I texted to let One know I was inside of the arena. From the court, he looked to the reserved seats and waved.

We sat side by side, kind of awkward at first, especially since we hadn't talked in several months. I didn't feel slighted that we hadn't talked. I'd been out in the world exploring my newfound freedoms. We watched a slow-paced youth game with limited conversation. Then One grabbed my hand. There is something to be said about hand holding. Hand holding seems completely innocuous, and mostly it can be. In the right context, it's entirely appropriate. But if I hadn't learned anything else from Duncan, I'd learned just how intimate, leading, or misleading a hand held can be.

Hands are often held in worship. Hands are held to congratulate and encourage. Hands are held to comfort. It's a loving display of affection, and children seem to do it without a second thought. I once knew a teenager who still held hands with her older sisters—their bond was honestly that deep. On the other hand (no pun intended) hand holding can be the "gateway touch," promoting connection and opening doorways for intimacy to exist where it otherwise would not. For that reason alone, it's good to exercise caution when handholding.

I guess I was out here being a handholding floozy because there I was, holding hands with One as he drew circles on my palm with his finger—some type of energy channeling, I'm convinced. After the game, we went to the concessions reserved for the VIP Suites. I had been to this arena many times throughout my life, but never in the VIP area. While taking in the crowded site, I spotted the mom of one of my best friends. I could not let her see me with an older man. I jerked my hand away, trying to hide. One looked at me for clarity. I nervously explained. He didn't respond. Here's the thing. My age was telling on myself and everyone involved. Nothing we do is hidden. As phrased by a man named Rod Pickens, *"Our lives testify against ourselves."*

My reaction was my red flag. While I could've defended that I was of legal age and technically an adult, I knew there were better expectations for me from those who knew me. Deep inside, I knew I was doing something I wasn't necessarily proud of. Otherwise, why hide? Similar to Duncan, One was in his mid-thirties, *or so he said*. If he overlooked my youth and immaturity, moments like, "Oh no, I can't let my best friend's mom see me!", surely should make a man rethink his life choices. We always have a way of escape.

Back at his hotel, we talked all night. I was sure to inquire about any relationships, this time not so casually, neither out of protocol, but with the intention to be sure never to repeat those haunting mistakes. No way would I relive last season's storm. One confirmed, repeatedly and with certainty, he was a single man. I really liked One; unlike with Duncan, I wasn't caught up in a tailspin. One liked me as well, and I caught the moment when he discovered he did. Like a light bulb switching on, he looked at me and said, "I like you." No overtures, just an honest observation. He was nothing like Duncan. One was gentle, reserved, and thoughtful.

We talked for what felt like hours. At some point, he tried to have sex. Although I liked him much more in a single day than I did the entire time with Duncan, I couldn't. I wouldn't. Even if I thought it was fate, we had just met. One of my coworkers would always laugh at my love for conscious hip-hop music. He'd say, "You think these men are so different. After they're finished talking deep, they still want more." He was right, but it wasn't going to happen. Besides, I was still emotionally healing. I didn't want a physically intimate relationship. Unlike with Duncan, I was able to quickly say no and honor myself in that manner. Unlike with Duncan, One didn't press the issue. We talked the night away.

Our conversation was interrupted by a knock on the door. One grabbed me as if to parade me along. Sadly, for me, on the other side of the door was a guy I previously worked with during my days interning at the marketing and promotions company. Although One and I were just hanging out, it wasn't a good look. The guy's face fell flat as if to say, "What are you doing in this man's room?!" He quickly looked away and continued with business. One was needed to handle logistics.

When One ran down to the lobby, I spun around in the hotel desk chair on cloud nine. It felt like something out of a fairy-tale. I literally learned of this man from a CD, he walks into my workplace weeks later, and there I was with him telling me he liked me. My guard was completely down, and I thought it was destiny that we'd be together. I looked out of the high-rise window and felt far from the reality I'd return to in the morning.

One opened the door, and seeing me next to the window, looked flushed.

"What are you doing?" He demanded sharply.

"Nothing. Looking out of the window." I was caught off guard by his tone.

His eyes darted toward his opened laptop on the desk in front of the window, which was now in front of me. He asked again. He thought I had violated his privacy—I had not. My head was too far in the clouds to think about his computer. I affirmed my truth. After a moment, he decided to believe me, and we resumed our date. I understood what it meant to be violated. Given the fact that he invited me into his space and left his belongings with me, I didn't take offense to his accusation. But should I have?

The next morning it was time for us to depart. He was heading back east, and I needed to get back to life. For the next three years, One and I had an emotional relationship. When he was in my city for business, we usually met. When he was away, we emailed and spoke over the phone. We never talked titles or boundaries. I was untethered and enjoying my single life, but it all paused whenever One was in town.

One day, a long-time friend of mine from the marketing and promo world, pulled me aside to have a word with me. He was laughing to offset his discomfort, but I could tell he was serious about whatever he was about to share.

"What? Say it!" I was curious about our random sidebar.

"Sonia. I know you're not out here like *this*, but your boy is telling everybody that he split your back wide open!"

"What?! We didn't do anything!" My tipster friend believed me and quite frankly didn't want to hear anything else about it. This particular friend was one of the many good guys in my life at that time. He and all the males I interned with had integrity. Not only were they intentional about not crossing boundaries, but also made responsible efforts to protect the boundaries the women they were around. I will forever appreciate these guys.

I couldn't believe One would act so immaturely. Spreading blatant lies about me to look cool, I suppose. Since he came off so deeply spiritual and reserved, I assumed he was above such immature behavior. *Wrong.* I emailed One to address the rumor. He evaded it by simply responding with a short deflection concluded with the word "LOVE." Shortly after, I received a book in the mail; bookmarked was a chapter entitled *Love,* followed by a music track named *Love.* Let's be honest. I *thought* I was in love. He knew it, played on it, and referenced it, but was in no way *"in love"* with me. I forgave the rumor.

My life during this time revolved around "free thinkers", chakras, and exploring spiritual boundaries. The way One and I met, through beat and lyric, I was convinced we were brought together for a purpose not yet realized. I ignored anyone who warned against engaging with energy practices, dismissing them as ill-informed and closed-minded. During conversations with One, we spoke a lot about racial and cultural identity. I read writings about African heritage and spirituality beyond religion. Although One was a Five Percenter, and I had no intentions of joining, I appreciated and considered his thoughts.

If he heard me use a term that was partially misunderstood, he'd offer a book title to help me gain a better understanding without belittling. We had a mutual respect for pursuing truth. There was a book I owned and cherished that supposedly taught the true identity of black people by dispelling widely accepted age-old myths. At the time, I regarded the book as my bible. In a random conversation, I quoted a line from the book.

"The cross is really an ankh with the symbol of the woman removed, leaving only the phallus."

"What did you say?" One was floored.

I happily repeated.

Irritated by my misinformed zeal, this Five Percenter schooled me on the Christian cross.

"The cross was originally two planks of wood used to crucify Jesus and others. There are a lot of people who do good and mean well for our culture, but you have to be careful—some people reach." In other words, anyone can publish opinions as facts and mislead an entire group while being equally misinformed.

I understood. It's not enough to read. We must critically think. A Five Percenter telling me that Jesus is real? I understood that the Islamic faith regards Jesus as a prophet, but personally hearing the practical testimony of Jesus' existence challenged my reality. One was not affirming Jesus to be his Lord, the Christ, or the Savior of the world. He simply affirmed the existence of Jesus, and for me, this changed my entire path.

The only information I conveniently read regarding Christianity was secondhand discourse, mostly refuting all religions. *Convenient* because, when we are not intentional, we tend to seek ideas that align with our currently held views. I appreciated that One shared the truth as he knew it without contorting it to suit himself. He wasn't throwing the historical existence of Jesus Christ under the bus because it didn't align with his personal views. It was simple; the cross was real and was really used on a real man named Jesus.

CHAPTER 8 | ONE & DONE

"…God is Love."
1 John 4:8 NLT

Life went on in its hustle and bustle. It had been three years since One and I first met. Our calls, emails, and meetings grew infrequent. The last time we saw each other, I knew with every ounce of my being it was our finale. As I departed in a cab I thought, *this is it*. I watched as the downtown lights transitioned into suburban lamp posts, and I couldn't shake the feeling. I didn't know how or why—I just knew it was over. Confirmation came in the form of an interview.

Interviewer: So, One do you have children?

God One: Without a doubt. I have a teenager and a newborn seed.

Interviewer: Are you married now?

God One: Yes, Sir!

Interviewer: Have you been married for a while?

God One: Forever(LOL)! The same sister since I was a youth. The same mother of my youth.

A wife? A newborn? It all made sense. From the frustrated guy who was with One the day we met at the record store to the look on my old colleague's face at the hotel. From One questioning me about his computer to the long breaks in our communication, the pieces fell together. One was indeed married, and others seemed to know as well.

Months after learning the truth, I saw a producer I knew from around the way whose studio I visited once with One. The producer casually asked if I'd spoken with One lately. I replied, "One was married." The producer looked at me blankly, seemingly caught off guard by my visible disgust. He responded matter-of-factly, "I thought you knew." *No. I didn't know.*

The night I found out, I paced my 300 sq. ft. apartment sorting thoughts. Was I naïve at eighteen, nineteen, twenty? Absolutely. Was I moving as straightforwardly and proactively as possible? Without a doubt. I had asked One several times if he had *any* relationship, *any* type of technicalities, with any woman.

Looking back, given the time we spent away from each other, I could've assumed he was lying. Still, a man's word is his bond, and he chose to lie. Haunted by my past, I constantly asked and was consistently told no. I guarded my body, making sure it wouldn't be bartered. Having gone through what I went through, I was adamant about not returning to it.

I didn't understand why One had involved himself with me, why he'd exploited my heart. What was he possibly getting in return? Why accept my love? I'm told the answers are evident to any man with a working member. But one and I never engaged in the act. He willingly pursued an emotional affair with me without my knowing it.

What we had was *nothing* to do with love. No surprise. I was taken captive by philosophy and empty deceit. I believed I was manifesting—with sheer willpower—my own divine destiny. Truthfully, I did not know Love.

By now, One was no longer answering my calls, which was his way of intentionally ending things. I've since learned, in general, to cut losses and quickly walk away without seeking a comforting conclusion. However, the younger me always needed answers, and there it was, in bold text on a show bill:

GOD ONE
'THE PEOPLE'S PARADIGM'
BLUEBERRY HILL'S DUCK ROOM, 7 P.M.

I showed up at the venue to let him know that he was exposed and with the idea of getting closure from some form of explanation. During soundcheck, One saw me and took five. He was tense and said, "Hey!" as if to say, "What are you doing here?"

"Congrats on your new baby."

He took a beat before mustering out a nervous, "Thank you," and then downed a glass of brown liquor, accidentally spilling it on my toes. I didn't even know he drank.

Whatever closure I was looking for, I quickly decided I wasn't going to get it and that I was better off leaving. I began to exit when a guy I knew from work ran up to me, excited.

"You know God One?" He was fangirling.

"Yeah," I scoffed. He wasn't a God—merely a man.

Welp, that's it. Out the door I went. With every step, old layers were being shed, and I was feeling liberated. The truth was the truth, and I was better off with it. A couple of blocks away, I turned back to look just one last time—at all that was and wasn't.

To my surprise, I saw One running out the door, looking to the left and the right. He seemed to be ready to offer an apology. From the other side of the street, I stopped and called out, "One!" The very moment I yelled, a jackhammer began drilling in the street, making it impossible for One to hear me. I waited for the hammer to stop and called out a second time. Immediately, just as before, the hammer began again. I laughed. I got it. It was time to go.

The absolute truth is that One never asked me to stop my clock for him. Later in life, a sister shared that

sometimes we give up way more than what is asked—
certainly more than others are willing to give—then
sulk at the roadblocks we've created for ourselves when
assumptions don't produce favorable outcomes.

Shortly following the whole ordeal, I had a dream. In
the dream, I was mortified to discover a person had
been harmed in a crime that I was somehow connected
to as a third party. Having no details, I was confused
about my involvement but felt deep sorrow for the
victim in the dream.

It may be obvious to you, but it wasn't so clear to
me. So, I shared the disturbing dream with an older
friend who passed it along to someone she knew and
trusted with dream insight. The dream mirrored what
had happened.

One was the perpetrator. His wife was his victim. I
was the unaware third party.

This weighed on my soul, irritating my spirit. The
truth that I was connected with anything that looked,
even slightly, similar to my days with Duncan—the
painful and shameful past I worked so hard to escape—
grieved me. It was personal. She didn't deserve it.

Chapter 9 | Arise O Ye Sleepers

"Ask, and it will be given to you; seek, and you will find;
knock, and it will be opened to you."
Matthew 7:7 ESV

I was immersed in the cool of the culture. As an informal student of the new age, I was indeed spiritual, however grossly unaware of the spirits I entertained. I thought Christians were blind sheep, foolishly following man. Christians claimed to have *the truth* but seemed far too attached to the things of this world and out of touch with their authentic selves.

The conscious community was full of people who seemed to love themselves, their culture, traditions, features, complexions, and textures. By contrast, Christians seemed artificially produced, presentable by societal standards, but disconnected from the awareness of being made in the image of God. Most Christians seemed like fakers, hiding behind suits, climbing a social ladder for personal agendas. Christians seemed to need a social club to fit into. These were my judgments.

Wisdom from an artist

For a short season, I hung out with Terrance, a guy I knew from high school. We were exclusively friends. He

83

was in a season of reinventing himself, and, feeling like an oddball myself, we clicked. Terrance needed to meet up with a friend one night, and I didn't mind driving. Claude, a talented muralist, wanted to use Terrance as a muse for a new work of art.

Claude's studio was covered with plastic and canvases when we arrived. As they talked, I sat patiently, taking in the paintings and pondering the meanings behind each piece. The two stood close by when I noticed Claude peer at me a few times in their conversation. It was not a look of interest, rather one of assessment. As they wrapped up their meeting, noticing my outfit, Claude had words for me.

Being heavy into identity, culture, and spirituality, I was always wearing some sort of a declarative statement. That night I wore all black with several Pan African symbols. From my t-shirt logo to my belt buckle and even a wrist band, I was ornamented in red, black, and green—the colors of the black liberation flag. Complementing the look were my shoulder-length locks adorned with cowrie shells. My overall look was loud and expressive, to say the least.

Claude began sharing something. I can't remember exactly what, but I got a strong impression that he was figuring out how to delicately word whatever he needed to say. After the patter, he, in the most tactful and respectful way, said plainly, "The revolution is bigger than the look."

Pow! Truth enveloped in grace shot out. I had sense enough to receive his wisdom. I wasn't offended, although I could have been. I felt no need to debate or defend myself, only receive. What he was saying was true. There is nothing wrong with representing a belief, but at what point does it go beyond a reference of representation to become a costume for a caricature?

In the same manner, a crook may wear clerical collars or loose women may appear modest; a look alone is not significant enough to define the spirit of a movement. When representation becomes performance, the intended purpose or message is lost. *The revolution is bigger than a look*. Those words, framed in grace, from a stranger, I'd never forget. That moment caused another pivot on my path.

I was on this journey, figuring out not only who I was but *whose I was*. I recall once, in my tiny apartment, how a series of random thoughts led me to say to myself, "I will *never* be a Christian." Immediately as the words left my mouth, my arms were covered with goosebumps. The sensation shocked me. It was like something out of a movie. I couldn't figure out why I got chills when I believed exactly what I was saying. On another occasion, alone in my apartment, something frightened me—maybe a noise. I had an eerie feeling in the pit of my spirit that wouldn't go away. I yelled, "Jesus!" I was absolutely not a Christian, nor did I believe in Jesus. I rolled my eyes, perturbed and puzzled as to why, of all names, I called out the name of Jesus.

Ever since the day One told me that Jesus was indeed a real person, I began my own research, but I still wasn't sure regarding deity. Before One, I hadn't considered Christ seriously since high school. Even with life now seemingly falling into place, I felt vacant. Something was missing that I couldn't quite put my finger on. My spirit was hungry for more. The enlightened culture-centric communities I hung out with were exciting, informative, charitable, relatively respectful, artistic, deeply spiritual, and filled with great people who were seemingly *free*— but it just wasn't *it*. I didn't know what *it* was that I was looking for, but this wasn't *it*.

I truly believed in an omniscient, omnipotent, and omnipresent God. A God that was indescribably good. But *Jesus*? I wasn't so sure. I figured that if God wanted me to know if the rumor of Jesus being the Christ were true, then God would have to show me. Based on what I'd heard, if God is a good God, then God would withhold no good thing from me. On that conviction, I asked with all sincerity.

"God, if Jesus is real, show me."

*"You will seek me and find me, when you seek me
with all your heart." (Jeremiah 29:13 NLT).*

But had I overlooked some things God had already shown me? I remembered a night while working in promotions. As moviegoers left the theater, I handed out flyers and music samples. I noticed a man who kept looking in my direction. From a distance, I observed he and a couple were enthralled in an intense conversation, and I wondered why he kept staring.

After a short time, the couple he spoke with seemed to be overcome with emotion and gratitude. With flushed faces, they thanked the gentleman profusely and waved goodbye. He started in my direction.

The ordinary-looking man began with small talk, questioning why men sagged their pants. I half-heartedly agreed, trying to understand his motives. Before long, he began sharing how God had never left him and how the Lord provided for his every need in the most miraculous of ways. He told me he was a prophet, was about the Lord's work, and because he worked for God, he never needed anything.

Looking at me, he said, "You get déjà vu a lot, don't you?"

I did! And in fact, I had just experienced it on my way to the theater that day.

"That's God." He said, then continued, "Give me a second." He ran to his car, which happened to be parked just a few feet away. After a moment he was back with—wouldn't you know it?—a large bag of red Twizzlers. "Want some?"

I did but was so shocked, I shook my head and said no. This stranger knew personal things about me and delivered a message with my favorite candy. He shared more things with me, including encouraging me to know that Jesus Christ was real and that Jesus knew all I was going through. He concluded with, "Go to church tomorrow. God has something for you."

That moment should have influenced me more. However, without having a personal relationship with Jesus Christ, the impact of that experience only lasted so long before the more exciting and intellectual things of the world offered seemingly better options. Nonetheless, I was still seeking, and it seemed as though God would speak directly.

Like that time I had a chat with my co-worker, Chanel. She praised Jesus while celebrating a small achievement, to which I naturally had nothing to add. I wasn't one of those vicious non-believers who vehemently attacked people of faith. Still, my silence must have announced the unspoken because she asked if I knew Jesus Christ.

Unashamed and proud, I told my truth. "I don't know Jesus," I said this matter-of-factly, not pitifully. While firm in my beliefs, I didn't desire to match wits or add what I thought I knew either. She was momentarily speechless, then invited me to visit with her at church. Chanel made it very clear. She wanted me to know that she wasn't treating me with any judgment. I accepted her invitation. I didn't mind visiting churches. Being open didn't mean I was converting.

Chanel's church was a small, old school, mom and pop style, sanctuary where a tiny congregation gathered each Wednesday night for Bible study. While waiting a short while for the pastor, a deacon ran onto the pulpit frazzled. He announced, "Pastor won't be joining us tonight, so I'll be leading the study. I didn't have a lesson planned, so let's open our Bibles and find out who this man named Jesus is."

Chanel and I looked at each other in awe. The message was clearly for me. The entire night was spent searching through scriptures to learn first-hand who Jesus Christ is. I would visit this church only a few more times. The Pastor encouraged me to continue in the way of the Lord through Jesus Christ and that there was a work to do, as the harvest is plentiful, and the laborers are few (Matthew 9:37 ESV). He encouraged me to keep asking, and that I would receive the answers I sought.

CHAPTER 10 | THE AWAKENING

"And you will know the truth,
and the truth will set you free."
John 8:32 NLT

Through these seemingly isolated events, God was setting me up for a wake-up. I eventually enrolled at Harris-Stowe State University, the first of a few attempts before completing a degree. One day my childhood friend, Cali, who attended a neighboring college, invited me to perform poetry for their annual BSA (Black Student Alliance) program. I enjoyed performing poetry, so I'd happily participate.

She then shared a small detail. "Afterwards, a group of us get together, hang out, and study the bible. Sometimes this *prophet woman* comes."

A Bible Study? Okay. Again, I was open. The majority of my high school friends were self-proclaimed Christians, so attending wouldn't be a problem. Interestingly, Cali wasn't one to be moved by prophecy. I always wondered if she included that part to bait me.

I agreed, but not for the prophet. I believed in my spirit I would eventually meet this woman if God desired, but I attended out of curiosity and for the fellowship. It felt safe hanging around students my age who were having fun but also taking proactive steps to seek God. It sounded like a good time to me.

The group was called Tru Impact; a small ministry affiliated with Impact, a national campus ministry. Once a week after rehearsal, a group of college-aged students would trickle in and study the Gospels of the Bible. Something was happening to me. During the studies, I could feel my spirit quickening. My heart was being pierced and all that I had come to know, challenged. I was hungry for the Word of God, for understanding, peace, and fellowship.

For the word of God is living and active and full of power. It is sharper than any two-edged sword, penetrating as far as the division of the soul and spirit, and of both joints and marrow exposing and judging the very thoughts and intentions of the heart. (Hebrews 4:12 AMP)

After a few weeks, I committed to regular attendance. One day a bright-eyed woman entered, and, without introduction, I knew exactly who she was. As she entered, my spirit took notice, and goosebumps danced on my arms, just as they had that day in my apartment. She carried some kind of anointing.

Minister Cici was an everyday woman who came in jeans and tennis shoes, no pious robe needed. She carried only the spirit of the Lord, the word of God, and a love for God's people. Her inviting smile showed she was equally excited to serve the young group. Her presence was beautiful.

We carried on with the Bible study as usual, but I was struggling this night. My spirit was sifting through all of the conflicting teachings I carried in the name of "being open." There was an intangible shift happening. My spiritual identity was changing without permission, and I wasn't sure if I was okay with it. I had once said, *"I'd never be a Christian,"* and I meant it.

Now, here I was receiving these words:

"I am the way, the truth and the life. No one comes to the Father except through Me" (John 14:6 NKJV).

Christians had been blind followers, in my opinion, and now my spirit was relentlessly leading me towards those I once regarded as fools.

"For the message of the cross is foolishness to those who are perishing, but to us who are being saved it is the power of God. For it is written: 'I will destroy the wisdom of the wise, and bring to nothing the understanding of the prudent.'" (1 Corinthians 1:19 NKJV).

93

One of the student leaders looked at me and asked if I was okay. Her concerned look told me that my valley of decision was written all over my face.

Amid crashing thoughts, I heard Minister Cici say, "You have a lot of questions, but you'll never know the answers if you never ask the questions." I nodded, knowing that, when confronted with the truth, there'd be no hiding behind popular opinion. I had to answer for myself.

"Who do you say I am?"

Jesus went out, and his disciples to the villages of Caesarea Philippi. And on the road, he asked his disciples, "Who do people say that I am?"

They answered him, "John the Baptist; others, Elijah; still others, one of the prophets."

"But you," he asked them, "Who do you say that I am? Peter answered him, "You are the Messiah." (Mark 8:27-29 CSB).

After the study, Minister Cici began speaking to us informally. She looked at Nathaniel, a brilliant academic, and told him he'd have no worries of money coming in his future. I was skeptical. He was extremely intelligent; the natural eye could perceive a lucrative future.

*Beloved, do not believe every spirit, but test the spirits
to see whether they are from God, for many false
prophets have gone out into the world* (1 John 1:4
ESV).

Minister Cici looked to Cali. I thought, "Okay, I'll
surely know if this woman is a swindler or not." I'd
known Cali since grade school.

Looking at Cali, she said, 'You know it's time for you
to come forward. You're a leader, but you're hiding."
Yup. That's about right.

She then looked at me and said these words, "Tell
them." I looked at her defiantly. I wasn't eager to tell this
room of folks, that I barely knew, my business. She
repeated, "Tell them." Not in logic, but in spirit, I
submitted.

The words tumbled out:
"Ilostmyvirginitytoamarriedman!"

My shame, spelled out in one abrupt run-on sentence.
But I said it. I had lost my virginity to a married man. The
words slapped everyone in the face. No one moved.

Cali, who had known me the longest, darted her eyes
toward me, then away quickly in total confusion and
possible disdain. Now, Duncan wasn't really married.
But for me, at that point, there was no distinction. Since

he was committed, or at least someone was committed to him, the impact on my life and the shame I carried was the same as if he had been. It was all filthy. I trespassed, and I was vandalized. I bore the shame of both, and it was the same kind of horrible. Technicalities didn't seem to matter much. This was the badge of shame that I carried for years. Those words I shouted back in the park, "I'll never forgive myself," survived.

Minister Cici didn't know what I was going to say—she was just following the leading of the Holy Spirit. I was being positioned to receive freedom. Because the atmosphere was authentically safe that night, I shared. To this day, I still have peace about sharing. Although at the moment, I was shocked that I told one of my deepest, darkest, scariest secrets. Not only I, but a young woman came to me that evening and shared that she carried a similar shame.

Psalm 124:7, "We have escaped like a bird from the snare of the fowlers; the snare is broken, and we have escaped!"

After Minister Cici spoke to a few more students, we all prayed and worshiped the Lord. The outpouring of the Holy Spirit was amazing, truly AWEsome. It was like a fresh rain cleansing us, individually and corporately. We were all spread out in the room, standing, kneeling, lying prostrate, whichever way the Spirit moved. Through it all, we worshiped our Heavenly Father.

Minister Cici floated around the room, moving from student to student, as the Spirit led her. She grabbed my hands to pray. I was already in tears. To this day, I still don't know how we ended up on the floor. I had never been so caught up in the Spirit that I didn't remember moving in the natural. On the floor, we were crying out in gratitude to God, sincerely giving thanks. She began saying something to me. Whatever it was, I thought within myself, *"God, I don't understand. You have to make it clear if you want me to get this."*

As I asked God for clarity, Minister Cici literally placed her ear to my chest as though she were listening to my heart. I'd never seen anything like it before that day or since. She firmly said, "Get up." Looking at me straight, she said plainly, "Stop having sex. God has plans."

It was indeed God confirming through Minister Cici what He had recently led me to do. About a week prior, I had been with a friend who wanted a relationship but not a commitment. After our last rendezvous, I left feeling especially empty. There was no joy or pleasure in what we'd be doing. I wanted a change.

"I'm not having sex anymore," I abruptly told him.

"All right," he responded, wanting to ask why but too prideful to.

This was bigger than him. Our temples were corroded. Like a decorated tomb, I was decent on the outside but inside, I was wayward, angry, unforgiving, and much more. God was using my emptiness to lead me to His fullness. Prophets often confirm what the Lord has already revealed to a person. Minister Cici's confirmation let me know that I was on the right path and not to backtrack on my previous decision. If there had been any margin left for me to change my mind in the coming days, this night—in worship—wiped it all away. Sex is communion between husband and wife, not a hobby between unmarried friends. I couldn't hang out in bondage and pursue freedom. So, in August of 2006, I walked away from a sexually promiscuous lifestyle and set out on a new journey by God's grace. But had I accepted Jesus? I'll get to that part.

CHAPTER 11 | 3 NIGHTS, 2 DREAMS

"For the weapons of our warfare are not carnal but mighty in God for pulling down strongholds…"
2 Corinthians 10:4 NKJV

Between Bible study, abstinence, workdays, and being enrolled in college, I was feeling pretty good. The Tru Impact Bible study was now an integral part of my new journey. I worshiped, prayed, and studied with an honest heart. My life was changing and seemingly for the better—but there was just one thing. When it came to Jesus, I was riding the wave of an experience and associations, but I had not committed. I had one foot in and one foot out.

Tru Impact was scheduled to street evangelize. T-shirts were being ordered, and I was happy to support in any way. But the day the shirt samples came in, I knew I was in trouble. Bright yellow t-shirts with red letters, boldly proclaimed, "Jesus Loves the Hell Out of You." I had never, in my life, represented the name, Jesus. My lifestyle, all I stood for and knew, was again being directly challenged by the Word, the name "Jesus."

With intention, the only symbol I had ever worn was an ankh—now I was preparing to wear a cross. I was at a crossroads. I enjoyed Bible study but was I ready to make a serious proclamation to the world affirming Jesus Christ as *my* Lord and Savior?

Deeply conflicted, those words, *"I'll never be a Christian,"* kept lingering. You may be thinking, how can someone attend a Christian Bible study regularly and serve the ministry without considering themselves a Christian? Easy, works of service have nothing to do with a surrendered heart. I had not accepted Jesus as my Lord (ruler of my life) or my Savior (a Redeemer providing salvation). While no one was pressuring me, and I was seemingly experiencing the regenerative power of the living Word, I was still unsure. Although the free fall ideology of *'anything goes—you only live once—do what makes you happy'* was no longer appealing, I still had questions.

I wasn't one to follow the majority. But I couldn't deny that something was changing within me as a result of studying the Bible. I invited the change. However, I was just fine with a small, quiet Bible study where only a select few knew me from a neighboring college. My life was being called into question, and I didn't think I was ready to answer.

You may also wonder how someone attends a Bible study faithfully, and no one ever questioned whether they're a believer in the God of the Bible. Well, Bible studies are for study, so I was given space to do just that.

From what I remember, there were no altar calls, so I wasn't called to make a formal declaration.

But there I was, being encouraged to loudly proclaim salvation through Christ on the street corners. Wearing the name Jesus was like waving a banner, and still, unsure of my salvation, I had never consciously decided to pick up the cross or count the cost.

I asked myself:

Do I stand for this?

Do I believe that Jesus died for my sins?

Is Jesus more than a prophet?

Am I now one of those I once reviled?

"Understand, Sonia," I told myself, "If you wear the shirt, you're going to be representing the testimony of Jesus Christ." I didn't take it lightly, but I didn't answer immediately either.

Compromise

I was basically shacking at the time, in other words, playing house. I knew shacking was improper, but I thought no harm was being done since I wasn't having sex and still had my own apartment. I was wrong. The simple truth is found in Genesis 2:24.

"…man leaves his father and mother and bonds with his wife, and they become one flesh."

Until we commit in marriage, we aren't called to be bonded with another *as one*. Singleness is such a special

101

time in our lives, but we often overlook it by chasing an idea, when in reality, we have no idea of the weighty call of marriage. During singleness, we're able to walk with our first love, the Lord, uninterrupted. It's a unique period of personal refinement that prepares and strengthens us for several pockets of life—including marriage.

One of the greatest lessons I've learned since this season, and am often reminded, is that the heart posture is just as important—if not more—as actions. Jesus says to the Pharisees, a group of self-righteous religious leaders, "Woe to you...hypocrites! For you are like whitewashed tombs that appear beautiful outwardly, but inside are full of...all uncleanness." (Matthew 23:27 NKJV). It is what God sees in us, not what others observe or say about us, that matters most.

One morning, my new beau, James, left before dawn for work. While still asleep, I heard footsteps on the living room carpet. I figured he'd forgotten something. I got up and followed the sound to the living room. To my surprise, he wasn't home. Odd? I laid back down. Moments later, I heard the sound of shuffling on the carpet again. Now the movement was closer to the bedroom I was in. I got up and checked the apartment. I knew for sure I'd heard something this time. Seeing nothing, I returned to rest.

Mid-sleep, I heard the sound of feet running towards me. Before I could get up, I was being attacked. I was now wide awake but couldn't completely open my eyes or move. My eyes must've been rolling because I saw flickers of light dash in and out of view. I could physically feel some form of resistance holding me down. After a seemingly long fight, it ended. I finally opened my eyes and stood up with my heart racing. Only, no one was in the room with me. Was it a nightmare? It couldn't have been. I was awake. I had never experienced anything like that before. It was indeed supernatural.

I would later learn the medical world calls this phenomenon "sleep paralysis" or a fear-based hallucination occurring around the time of sleep. Some church folks call it 'witches riding your back.'

I told James about the bizarre experience, but he was just as clueless about it as I was. About a week later, he was attacked in the same manner. Hindsight tells me that our unofficial shacking and inappropriate canoodling may have aided in the access of an open doorway for the dark intruder.

A friend of James, Marvin, was raised as a Christian and familiar with demonic attacks. He told us to "plead the blood of Jesus" if it were to happen again. In other words, we were to call on the saving power of Jesus Christ. This confession, in the face of a demon who was invoking fear and taking up territory, would proclaim that Jesus Christ shed blood for our sins. Thus, the demon would have to flee by having no legal ground.

What we weren't understanding was that, based on Marvin's instruction, *this enemy actually had legal ground.* Although I spent time with Christians and even served in some capacity, I had not personally accepted Jesus as my Lord and Savior, so how could I proclaim His blood to cover me?

I had previously dabbled in the esoteric but never had I experienced a real demonic attack. Never! I was petrified that this was really happening. But why now? My budding relationship with Jesus was the only difference. The demonic attack worked through intimidation, and I believe God allowed it. Partly because I needed to examine my faith— *"Choose you this day whom ye will serve"* (Joshua 24:15 KJV).

Shortly after the attack, I had a dream.

I was leaving James' apartment. I didn't want to but knew I needed to. He questioned if we were breaking up. I confirmed we were not, but that I had to go. I saw Cali from Bible study, she felt like a strong support. I drove home.

I woke up and knew without a doubt I needed to leave James' apartment, although I didn't want to. At some point during the day, I let him know that I was leaving. Just like in the dream, he asked if we were breaking up. We weren't.

I had spent so much time with James that I basically had let one of my friends, Abby, live at my apartment. I came home that day unexpectedly, surprising her. I should have given her a heads up, but my mind was all over the place. Sadly, I hadn't considered her. She laid on the couch, and I laid on the floor wondering about the spiritual pull I was feeling. Things were shifting in a way that I could not articulate. It was like the wind. I couldn't see it or grab it, but I felt it.

We both started to fall asleep. I was lying about a foot from the front door when I thought, "It would be so creepy if someone knocked on the door." Not even a minute later—knock, knock. Abby and I looked at each other puzzled. Who would be knocking at this hour? Generally, no one came by unannounced. I was full of fear and placed my finger over my mouth to signify to Abby to try to keep quiet. I never opened the door.

Later that night, I slept on the couch while Abby was welcome to the bedroom. I was attacked again. Every time I closed my eyes, I had an overwhelming sensation of fear. Not too long after, I could feel that unfamiliar presence, and then my eyes would roll mid-sleep before

I'd fight to fully wake up. I was scared out of my mind and frustrated that I couldn't get rest. The attacks were eerie and intimidating.

After several attacks and not knowing what to do, I called Marvin, who had initially told us to plead the blood of Jesus. Out of respect, I'd normally never call a boyfriend's friend. But I felt like this was life and death. I called the only person I knew who'd have an answer. In a way, this was spiritual life and death. I shared that the attacks were ongoing and whispered as I told Marvin I didn't want Abby to think I was crazy.

He nonchalantly laughed throughout the call as if what I was going through was nothing. He said it wasn't good that I had someone over because I didn't know what spirits were attached to them and not to be afraid. I was to read the Word of God, praise, pray, and keep pleading the blood of Jesus. The demons should then leave me alone.

"That's it?" I wondered. But I *was* pleading the blood of Jesus, and it wasn't working. How was I not supposed to be afraid? I *was* afraid, and I could sense this enemy's excitement, enticed by my fear. How do I turn instinctual fear off? It is said that you can't prepare for a fight, in a fight. I was losing against an unseen enemy who apparently could see me. There's nothing like searching for help in a situation where only God can help you. Very humbling. Abby overheard me talking, and after I got off

the phone, very sweetly said, "You know Sonia, you can tell me anything. I won't think you're crazy."

That night I slept in the bed with Abby, and rest finally came. Abby was a believer. I'm not sure why I didn't let her in on the details. I guess I didn't know who to trust with this bizarre experience. Abby left after a few days. She may have been being considerate of me or simply needed her own space. I didn't want her to leave, but I didn't bother to stop her after receiving the advice about spiritual attachments.

Fear of Sleeping

The next few days would open my eyes. During the day, all was well. But after nightfall, fear filled my heart. I'd stay up as long as I could to avoid sleep. I would read the Word and play worship music. Still, there was a layer of tangible fear in the atmosphere. As I started dozing off, boom—an attack! As instructed, I'd plead the blood of Jesus and read Psalm 91.

> *"You will not fear the terror of the night,*
> *nor the arrow that flies by day,*
> *nor the pestilence that stalks in darkness,*
> *nor the destruction that wastes at noonday."*
> Psalm 91:5-6 ESV

Yet again, as soon as I closed my eyes, another attack. Exhausted, I sat up and reached for the lamp. A little light would provide comfort. When I turned the switch, the light bulb not only blew out but exploded with broken glass flying over my head. Maybe the bulbs were cheap, but it sure was coincidentally strange. I pleaded the blood of Jesus and decided to avoid sleep altogether.

I didn't sleep for three nights. I didn't know my body could go on that long. I was like a walking zombie during the day, and still not sure how I got through morning classes. On the third night, I struggled the same as before, but sleep was getting the better of me. As soon as my eyes closed, I was attacked. I woke up again, but not for long. I couldn't fight sleep and had two dreams.

Dream One

I was standing in a dark room with two other people, one to my left and the other to my right. I couldn't see their faces but felt their presence. Directly in front of us was a sinister figure. I saw only eyes—evil eyes. This evil figure held a Bible. It passed the Bible around, starting with the person to my right. The person to my right read a scripture aloud. The evil one placed the Bible before me. I was too afraid to read the Word aloud. The eyes looked cunningly pleased. It continued to rotate the Bible among the three of us. It came back to me a second time, holding the Bible in front of me to read the Word aloud. Again, with the Word before me, I was too afraid to speak it. Immediately, the evil figure lunged toward me.

I woke up struggling to free myself from this spiritual attack manifesting physically.

Dream Two

I was running for my life through a town square. I was being chased by an evil enemy. I ran into a high-rise building that had different establishments within it. I was terrified for my life. I could only catch glimpses of the enemy chasing me—sinister eyes were all I saw. I ran into the bathroom to hide before escaping to the highest floor. Now, looking at a window before me, I was out of options. There was nowhere further to run.

I turned around to see the enemy chasing me, but it stopped right at the doorway of this upper room. The dark presence stared at me with the evilest look and then went on its way.

God graciously gave those two dreams, showing me a glimpse of His power, my heart, and the intent of the enemy. The Lord was teaching me how to fight a spiritual battle. I learned a few things from those dreams.

The Word of God is a Weapon

Hebrews 4:12 reads, *"For the word of God is alive and powerful. It is sharper than the sharpest two-edged sword, cutting between soul and spirit, between joint and marrow. It exposes our innermost thoughts and desires."*

I had previously been taught that the Bible was a tool of manipulation used to keep people bound. The Lord was showing me that in this kind of spiritual battle, victory, power, and authority come *through the Word of God*. By not speaking the Word, I was giving the enemy territorial ground over my life. *There is power in the living Word of God.*

Know the Word

The enemy knows the Word of God and also knew that I did not. The enemy is a tormentor who will harass you like a gnat and intimidate you like a roaring lion, but the enemy cannot touch you *if you are under the covering of God through Jesus.* God is merciful.

"Every word of God is pure: he is a shield to those who put their trust in him."
Proverbs 30:5 KJV

The Lord is a Strong Tower

In the second dream, notice that I ran to the bathroom, and once in the upper room, the enemy never entered. Bathrooms signify a place of cleansing. I desperately needed cleansing in every area of my life. A process of cleansing would be a major role in experiencing victory over the traps of the enemy.

In the Old Testament, the upper room represents the presence of God and was found in the dwellings of the wealthy. This would apply spiritually here. In the New Testament, the upper room relates to prayer and fellowship. Along with the Word of God, God's presence and relationship, personal spiritual cleansing, prayer, fellowship, and continually seeking spiritual riches, victory would be mine.

I was given a blueprint, a road map, for victory. The enemy, that is the satan—which in Hebrew means adversary—comes like a roaring lion to steal, kill and destroy. But God was working on my behalf. We can't just speak the Word; we must *know* the Word and then live the Word. Even the enemy knows the word of God. The Bible says the enemy used the Word to tempt Jesus in the wilderness. "Even the demons believe in the word of God and tremble," says James 2:19.

I knew God was calling me in a direction I had never seen for myself. But would I trust Him enough to take

His hand and follow? I had asked plainly, "Is Jesus real?" In more ways than one, God answered. In the most loving and personal way, God showed me that all I had known was wrong. From those sleepless nights and revelatory dreams, I knew satan was angry that I was walking toward Jesus Christ with a pure heart. The scales were falling, and skepticism faded behind a new personal faith.

I finally knew and fully believed that *Jesus Christ is real*. I also knew that I'd been entertaining the dark side, in many ways unknowingly. When I had studied various and conflicting spiritual beliefs, there were never any attacks. When I denounced Jesus, no attacks. Fornicated, no attacks. When I reveled in drunkenness, no attacks. Played around with the esoteric; palm reading, astrology, and trance meditation, no attacks.

But the moment I laid it all down and began to let Jesus into my heart, chaos broke loose. Not once in all my dabbling with the occult did I ever experience a demonic attack manifested in such an overtly threatening way where I knew without a shadow of a doubt there was a dark entity gunning for me. Not ever. Never before Christ. Yes, Christ is real and had been grossly misunderstood by me.

Why was I never attacked when dabbling in the dark arts? Because I was, unknowingly, on the enemy's side.

"If a kingdom is divided against itself, that kingdom cannot stand." (Mark 3:24 NKJV).

I was convinced, after the attacks, that most folks who call themselves "spiritual" have no idea of the literal spirits that are actually being entertained or battled. I understood that my eyes were being opened to the truth that I'd once rejected. Jesus Christ exists. The enemy knows it also and was directly attacking the revelation of Jesus Christ as the risen and living Lord and Savior from being received.

God, now I believe. Jesus, I receive You. It was time to get my house in order. Soon after that experience, I took a big trash bag and looked around my dimly lit apartment. Where do I begin? A beautifully carved Buddha statue, the *Book of the Dead,* an astrology guide, and a picture I'd long sensed had a dark spiritual force attached to it. I bagged the items up, along with a few other trinkets, and trashed them.

Interestingly, there is a similar occurrence in the nineteenth chapter of the book of Acts. God was performing amazing miracles through the hands of the Apostle Paul. Some traveling Jewish exorcists witnessed the move of God and began using the name of Jesus, like a magic formula, without having a personal revelation of or relationship with Christ. This is what I was doing. Those nights I used the name of Jesus to protect me. Nothing was happening because I didn't know Jesus and

113

hadn't accepted Him into my life. I just wanted a quick deliverance.

The chapter further goes on to mention the seven sons of a high priest named Sceva. These sons also did the same by imitating Paul in using the name of Jesus. The Word says, "The evil spirit answered them, "I know Jesus, and I recognize Paul—but who are you?' The man who possessed the evil spirit prevailed against them, and the seven sons ran away naked and wounded. When this wild event spread throughout the city of Ephesus, many who became believers repented of their practices and burned their sorcery books. My home, much like myself, needed cleansing.

Chapter 12 | New Dawn

"Yes, I have loved you with an everlasting love;
Therefore with lovingkindness I have drawn you."
Jeremiah 31:3 NKJV

I started attending *club church*, the nickname I gave it once I eventually saw it for what it was. This popular St. Louis County church was where a lot of babes in Christ went, in part because it had a large following. As a babe in Christ, the milk given was good for a time. The word gave me just enough to mull over from week to week.

Shortly after joining, I was invited by the church to sign up for baptism. I initially declined. The woman on the phone seemed confused about my objection but didn't push me to agree. At the time, I thought being baptized was a mere tradition with no real spiritual impact, being more symbolic than necessary. I was extremely cautious about partaking in religion. I had just received Christ into my life, and I was working hard to keep the traditions of man out.

The following week, a different minister called to invite me to sign up for baptism. This minister challenged my position with a short explanation of the purpose of baptism. Baptism is the act of dying to self, being buried, and raised. Just as Christ died to self to do the Father's will, so do we die to self in the name of Jesus (see Romans 6). My understanding had been sincere but wrong. I scheduled my baptism for two weeks out, fully ready to cancel if needed. Two older women, counselors that I knew personally, both gave me resources to read so that I could make a personally informed decision.

My spirit was at peace; I would get baptized. Days ahead, all of the baptism candidates met to rehearse for the service, which was a bigger procession than I anticipated. Together, we sat in the pews watching the choir rehearse. While enjoying the worship, I saw a bright glow in my peripheral vision. I quickly looked to the light, but immediately it was gone; I only saw a woman singing in the choir. I brushed it off and went back to praising. As soon as I looked away, the illumination returned. Quickly looking towards the woman, the light disappeared again.

On the night of the baptism, I was nervous, and unsure why. Maybe because I was taking real steps towards a real conversion. A sister attended, but I still felt alone on my journey—so much of the unknown lay ahead.

After I was dunked in the water, my spirit was full, and I shed tears privately—it was indeed a spiritual act. As service was dismissing, I began walking up a crowded aisle to leave. A little ahead of me, a woman stopped walking. She turned around, stared at me a moment, then smiled before continuing out the door. It was her, the woman in the choir with the peculiar glow. For the duration of my time attending the church, I never saw her again. I don't know what the light was about, but it felt like one of those moments where God uses others to say, "I see you."

Back at work, I sat at my cubicle, twiddling my hair in between calls. Holding a single dreadlock, I noticed several tiny white fuzzies woven throughout. Upon further observation, it was evident that dust and other particles were attached to my strands. Locks are formed by the intertwining of the natural curl pattern with minimal manipulation. As beautiful as they are, by nature they attract unwanted elements and, when not properly protected or maintained, these elements become interwoven within the growth process. It was evident that my regime hadn't been enough.

The first thing that came to mind were remnants of my past: waywardness, men, a life without Christ. The old me was still with me, literally. It was time to let it go.

At my bathroom sink, section by section, snipped locks fell to the floor along with memories of what they once meant to me. When I first started the natural hair journey, it defined me. But now, I was a different young woman, no longer defined by a look or that season of life.

This is not a slight against the hairstyle. The significance was plainly more spiritual than physical. All

I knew was that for me, the old had passed, and the new had come.

Hello New Day! I Thank God for You.

Excited about experiencing true freedom, I shared my testimony with a couple of friends along the way; not the surface level testimonies we tend to give when trying to maintain a level of superficial righteousness, but the ugly testimony that gives God all of the glory. One of these friends was back home visiting from college when she shared with me her attempt to break up a deeply committed young couple who'd just transferred to her campus. She was so smitten by the young man that she wondered if she could lure him away. In hearing, I said, "Don't do that. That's wrong." Mildly defensive, she casually reminded me of my past. This taught me about being intentional with sharing. Testimonies are great tools of encouragement for both the hearer and the sharer, but if not communicated clearly, the wrong message is caught, and the fruit of the story is lost. Duncan was a one-time mistake that cost me greatly, not a lifestyle. A one-time mistake. That situation had been years past and never repeated. I shared my testimony, not to validate causing another person harm but to glorify God's goodness and unmerited love for us despite our lowliness. I shared because I was set free. Her response floored me. *What part of my 'testimony' did she miss*? I was far from perfect, but I wasn't with the mean girl treachery. Needless to say, for other reasons, our friendship didn't stand the test of time.

If we confess our sins, he is faithful and just to forgive us our sins and cleanse us from all unrighteousness. (1 John 1:19 KJV)

I quickly learned that this new walk wasn't exactly an easy one. But it was transformative, deeply fulfilling, sometimes lonely, other times overwhelming, and many times, challenging. Easy? No such thing. There's a fitting scripture.

"Enter by the narrow gate; for wide is the gate and broad is the way that leads to destruction, and there are many who go in by it. Because narrow is the gate and difficult is the way which leads to life, and there are few who find it." (Matthew 7:13-14 NKJV).

Matthew 7 spells it out perfectly. What I once criticized as Christians blindly following religious rules was to the contrary often intentional and circumspect living, *"...for wide is the path that leads to destruction, and there are many who go in by it."* Long gone were the days of throwing caution to the wind by embracing the bliss of ignorance. *"My people perish for a lack of knowledge,"* says the Lord in Hosea 4:6 (KJV).

Sometimes you have to go the path alone. People didn't always understand what was going on with me, and I had to be okay with that in order to take the next steps. The tables had turned. I was now being debated or dismissed for believing in "lies" and, on one occasion, experienced mildly aggressive opposition during campus evangelizing. Some relatives scoffed at my spiritual journey, and some friends simply didn't find me as fun. When I cut off my locks, there were those who embraced it while others ridiculed. I remember thinking, I don't need permission to change.

I do understand change can be uncomfortable, but I realized that some people sometimes define themselves only by who they are in relation to another. Some feel smarter standing next to the uneducated, more accomplished as long as they're the one with the better career, or more valuable as long as they know another is in a struggle. Some people, as long as you don't change, like having you around; they may even like you better bound. Freedom begets freedom. The moment you change, for the better or worse, your environment and those in it are indirectly influenced.

I once was blind; now I see, and there is so much to see, more than I could ever see in a thousand lifetimes. Obedience to the indwelling Holy Spirit has never been about mind control, spiritual domination, or gross manipulation. Rather, it's the protection of our precious souls and a testament of our trust in the Lord's immeasurable force of love.

This is the love I had been chasing my entire life. A holy love. A divine and pure love. A deep love. An incomprehensible, unintelligible, soul-stirring, life-shaking love. A protective, "I will never leave you nor forsake you," love. A proactive, "Against all odds, I will seek you, find you, keep you, from now until eternity," kind of love. An "I will cleanse you through My love, cover you with My love because I Am love," kind of love. This is *real* love. And I tasted it. I had to have it and always want more from the true Source.

Anything else is not enough. This new walk is beautifully complex yet so simple. I love the Lord because the Lord first loved me. I could not have known true love unless the Lord first showed me.

Walking with the Lord was like stepping into a new world. Interestingly, the more we walk together, the more the Lord unearths, revealing His fingerprint in every detail. The more I learn, the more I understand how little I know. The closer we get, the clearer I see how far and wide the Lord's love flows. As the Apostle Paul writes—

"And I am convinced that nothing can ever separate us from God's love. Neither death nor life, neither angels nor demons, neither our fears for today nor our worries about tomorrow—not even the powers of hell can separate us from God's love. No power in the sky above or in the earth below—indeed, nothing in all creation will ever be able to separate us from the love of God that is revealed in Christ Jesus our Lord." (Romans 8:38-39 NLT).

The better it gets, the harder the walk, but the harder the walk, the sweeter the fruit. What do I mean? As with olives, the pressing produces the oil; diamonds and pearls alike gain value from pressure. It is in the refiners' fire that silver and gold are tested. This was only the beginning.

My character is constantly being stretched, called to grow more in the Lord—deeper, wider, higher. Each season is new and unpredictable, some hard and ugly, others, refreshing and joyful. I anchor myself with hope in the Lord. When times get unbearably tough, and prayers seem long and unheard, the Lord shows Himself in unexpected ways, reminding that He is the Potter, and I am the clay. God will not be directed, mocked, or boxed; yet, we can trust Him.

When we pray, "Remove it, Lord." Or, "Take the pain!"

Jesus says, "My grace is sufficient." (2 Co 12:9 KJV).
When we ask, "How much longer, Lord?"
We're able to preserver with His words, "I will *never*
leave you nor forsake you." (Heb 13:5 ESV).

That's easier said than done, but the Lord loves us so
much. So much—as we are, where we are, no matter
what we've done. Looking back, what some saw as a set-
up for failure was actually a set-up for a blessing. My
canvas began blank. God used—and still uses—every
opportunity to paint His eternal truth, an unadulterated
and remarkable truth. The truth that doesn't need me to
believe in order for it to be true. The truth is that Jesus
was born. Jesus died for our sins. Jesus rose, and He's
coming again! The truth is that one day we will all come
face to face with the Truth, and every knee shall bow, and
every tongue shall confess that He is Lord.

During His ministry, Jesus was criticized for eating
with sinners, to which He replied:

*"Healthy people don't need a doctor—sick people do. I
have come to call not those who think they are
righteous, but those who know they are sinners"* (Mark
2:17 NLT).

I know I'm a sinner—I'm not jealous of divinity. Born
of flesh, in a fallen state, our bodies will one day decay.

123

That's a fact. On that day, do you know where your soul is going? I won't belabor the point. Heaven is *real*, and so is hell. I know you can't believe just because I tell you. God has to show you, and I'm confident the Lord will. I can't assume where you are in your spiritual walk. You may be further along than I—and there's no competition, by the way. But, if you're in a place where you just don't know about the man named Jesus, if you have a million and one questions, struggle with who and what to believe but you want the *truth*, I'm standing in the gap for you.

Lord, Jesus, You know what we don't. You have the power and authority to do what we can't. For the one honestly wondering if You are real, if You are the Way, the Truth, and the Life, and if eternal salvation comes only by You, please show them as only You can. Thank You, Lord, for your love and faithfulness. Amen.

Life Has Just Begun

> *"AWAKE, O SLEEPER, AND ARISE FROM THE DEAD, AND CHRIST WILL SHINE ON YOU"*
> (Ephesians 5:14 ESV).

Through a series of divinely orchestrated events, I came to a point where I had no other choice but to choose the Truth before me. God chased me with LOVE because of His MERCY. In His sovereignty, He relentlessly pursues, warns, and protects.

"Mom, is God real?" A suspicious child asked. Mom was on a search of her own, looking for words she deemed right and responsible.

With a blindsided and flat expression, she offered, "I can't answer that for you. You'll have to find out on your own."

I found out.

"Fear not, for I have redeemed you; I have called you by name. You are Mine."
Isaiah 43:1 ESV

PSALM 91 - MY REFUGE AND MY FORTRESS

He who dwells in the shelter of the Most High
will abide in the shadow of the Almighty.
I will say[a] to the Lord, "My refuge and my fortress,
my God, in whom I trust."
For He will deliver you from the snare of the fowler
and from the deadly pestilence.
He will cover you with His pinions,
and under His wings you will find refuge;
His faithfulness is a shield and buckler.
You will not fear the terror of the night,
nor the arrow that flies by day,
nor the pestilence that stalks in darkness,
nor the destruction that wastes at noonday.
A thousand may fall at your side,
ten thousand at your right hand,
but it will not come near you.
You will only look with your eyes
and see the recompense of the wicked.
Because you have made the Lord your dwelling place—
the Most High, who is my refuge[b]—
no evil shall be allowed to befall you,
no plague come near your tent.
For He will command His angels concerning you
to guard you in all your ways.
On their hands they will bear you up,
lest you strike your foot against a stone.
You will tread on the lion and the adder;
the young lion and the serpent you will trample underfoot.
"Because he holds fast to Me in love, I will deliver him;
I will protect him, because he knows My name.
When he calls to Me, I will answer him;
I will be with him in trouble;
I will rescue him and honor him.
With long life I will satisfy him
and show him My salvation."

Footnotes

Psalm 91:2 Septuagint *He will say*

Psalm 91:9 Or *For you, O Lord, are my refuge! You have made the Most High your dwelling place*

https://www.biblegateway.com/passage/?search=psalm+91&version=ESV

www.ingramcontent.com/pod-product-compliance
Lightning Source LLC
Chambersburg PA
CBHW071156120626
46546CB00006B/2286